Beginning Cataloging

Beginning Cataloging

JEAN WEIHS
Technical Services Group
Toronto, Canada

and

SHEILA S. INTNER
Professor Emerita
Simmons College Graduate School of Library and
Information Science at Mount Holyoke College
South Hadley, Massachusetts

LIBRARIES UNLIMITED
An Imprint of ABC-CLIO, LLC

A B C 🞉 C L I O

Santa Barbara, California • Denver, Colorado • Oxford, England

Library of Congress Cataloging-in-Publication Data

Weihs, Jean Riddle.
  Beginning cataloging / Jean Weihs, Sheila S. Intner.
    p. cm.
  Includes bibliographical references and index.
  ISBN 978-1-59158-687-6 (acid-free paper). — ISBN 978-1-59158-839-9
(pbk: acid-free paper) 1. Cataloging. 2. Classification—Books. I. Intner,
Sheila S. II. Title.
  Z693.W45 2009
  025.3—dc22   2009016011

13 12 11 10 9 1 2 3 4 5

This book is also available on the World Wide Web as an eBook.
Visit http://www.abc-clio.com for details.

ABC-CLIO, LLC
130 Cremona Drive, P.O. Box 1911
Santa Barbara, California 93116-1911

This book is printed on acid-free paper ∞

Manufactured in the United States of America

Contents

1

Introduction

This book was written to convey knowledge about standard methods of cataloging and classifying library materials. It is intended as a beginner's introduction and does not attempt to be exhaustive.

As this book's title states, it was written for beginning catalogers, those who are students in library technician programs and in teacher-librarian programs, and for others who do not have formal training in cataloging but find themselves in situations where cataloging must be undertaken. The text can also be effectively used as a workbook for students in cataloging courses at faculties of information studies. It may also help people in reference departments or students studying reference skills to have an understanding of the catalog.

Standardized Cataloging

The public catalog is the most important tool patrons can use to find what the library has both in its local collection and its remote access collection. Public catalogs can enable searchers to see what materials are available by particular authors or on subjects of interest as well as what versions and editions of a title can be found in the collections.

Standardized cataloging is the key that opens the door of better access to local materials— materials that can satisfy patrons' information, recreation, and education needs. Standardized cataloging not only enables local catalogs to perform better for their users, but also makes it possible for the local catalog to link more effectively with the other catalogs belonging to the same bibliographic network. These links might be to catalogs in public libraries, media centers, colleges and universities, special libraries, state and provincial libraries, and national libraries. Standardized cataloging also makes it possible to understand the bibliographic records in foreign-language libraries. The ultimate goal is to make any title owned anywhere in the world available to a person with a need for that material.

Good cataloging also contributes to the use of materials by making it easier for those searching the catalog to find what they want and need. A catalog containing high quality, standardized information gives better responses to searchers' queries. Standard methods can be applied to all sorts of information resources in all kinds of physical forms. Searchers are prepared for encounters with catalogs and collections in college, university, and corporate libraries when they have used a good quality catalog in their local public libraries and school media centers.

With few exceptions, all libraries use standard tools to catalog their collections. These tools allow a library to use sources of catalog copy from other databases or from cataloging-in-publication (CIP) for a local catalog—an effective way of reducing the costs of cataloging.

Functions of the Catalog

Charles Ammi Cutter, one of America's most distinguished and innovative librarians, published America's first book of rules for cataloging materials in 1876, establishing the purpose of catalogs as follows:

1. To enable a person to find a book when one of the following is known:
   a) the author
   b) the title
   c) the subject.

2. To show what the library has
   d) by a given author
   e) on a given subject
   f) in a given kind of literature.

3. To assist in the choice of a book
   g) as to the edition (bibliographically)
   h) as to its character (literary or topical).

Cutter called these purposes "the objects of the catalog." They have been valid for more than 130 years and continue to express what current catalogs try to achieve.[1]

Cutter's objects describe two distinct functions for the catalog: a finding list function and a collocation (gathering) function. Patrons who approach the catalog with a known item in mind are served by the finding list function. When they search for the item, the presence or absence of a record for it in the catalog informs them if it is part of the collection. If patrons are unsure of an exact item, but want to select an item from among the works of an author, or find a particular edition of a work, or locate materials on a subject, the collocation function gathers all the records that match a chosen search term and helps to answer their queries. All the publications of an author are filed in one place under the heading for the author's name, all the editions of a work are filed together under the heading for the title, and all the publications on a subject are gathered under the headings for that subject. Searchers can scan the set of records gathered under their search terms (name, title, or subject) and select what they want.

Further Learning

People who have mastered the contents of this book, which deals with the cataloging of books, and want more in-depth knowledge in both book and nonbook cataloging can move on to *Standard Cataloging for School and Public Libraries*, which deals with both book and nonbook materials in more depth.[2] *Organizing Audiovisual and Electronic Resources: A Cataloging Guide* is also recommended to those wishing more focused instruction on the cataloging of audiovisual materials and online electronic resources.[3] *Cataloging Audiovisual Materials and Other Special Materials: A Manual Based on AACR2 and MARC 21* is a useful handbook for the cataloging of nonbook materials.[4]

Blank pages with the heading "Additional Information" are available at the end of each chapter for a cataloger to add to the knowledge in this book as she or he becomes more proficient in cataloging and has learned to consult some of the sources listed at the end of subsequent chapters. Such personal notes may occur when a cataloger regularly encounters a more complex type of material than is discussed in this book or when *RDA: Resource Description and Access* (see page 31) is implemented in the next decade.

A Word About the Figures and Exercises

The figures in Chapters 2 to 7 highlight a student's progress in learning to catalog. While no textbook can supply all the practice students might want or need to polish their cataloging and classification skills, exercises are provided at the end of each chapter, from chapters 3 to 7, to enable readers to apply the tools discussed within the chapters.

The figures in Chapter 2 illustrate the CIP information usually found on the verso of most books because CIP is frequently the basis on which catalog records are built. The figures and exercises in Chapters 3 to 6 are done in the format used in CIP, the traditional cataloging format, because it is easier to demonstrate cataloging principles building on CIP records without the distraction of computer encoding. In Chapter 7, "Computer Coding," the figures and exercises contain standard MARC (MAchine Readable Cataloging) coding. The subfield codes in these records have been separated from the terms followed by a space to make the coding more understandable to the beginning cataloger. The MARC exercises in this book do not require students and novice catalogers to code many of the fixed fields, because fixed fields are handled differently by various data banks. A graduate cataloger will learn the needs of a library's system on the job.

The figures and exercises in Chapter 3, "Descriptive Cataloging," do not include "tracings," that is, the subject headings and additional descriptive headings that are added to the records in the course of normal cataloging procedures. When the beginning cataloger progresses to Chapter 4, "Access Points," the figures and exercises will include tracings for the added entries prescribed in *Anglo-American Cataloguing Rules*. Subject headings are added to the tracings in the figures and exercises in Chapter 5 and call numbers to the bibliographic records in Chapter 6, "Classification." At this point the bibliographic record is complete. In Chapter 7, the beginning cataloger learns to code this complete bibliographical record in the MARC format so that it can become part of an online public access catalog (OPAC).

Double hyphens (--) have been used in place of dashes in the figures and answers to the exercises because it is easy for beginners to confuse single hyphens and dashes.

Answers to the examples in the exercises can be found in the appendices at the end of the book. The authors believe it is not difficult to do high quality, standard cataloging. It just takes the right knowledge, a little confidence, and practice.

Notes

1.   Charles A. Cutter, *Rules for a Dictionary Catalog*, 4th ed. Washington, DC: Government Printing Office, 1904, 12. Reprints of Cutter's "functions" can be found in many more currently published books. For a fuller explanation, see pages 62–71 in *Foundations of Cataloging: A Sourcebook*, edited by Michael Carpenter and Elaine Svenonius. Littleton, CO: Libraries Unlimited, 1985, which should be available in library science collections.

2.   Sheila S. Intner, and Jean Weihs, *Standard Cataloging for School and Public Libraries*, 4th ed. Westport, CT: Libraries Unlimited, 2007.

3. Ingrid Hsieh-Yee, *Organizing Audiovisual and Electronic Resources: A Cataloging Guide*, 2nd ed. Westport, CT: Libraries Unlimited, 2006.

4. Nancy B. Olsen with the assistance of Robert L. Bothmann and Jessica J. Schomberg, *Cataloging of Audiovisual Materials and Other Special Materials: A Manual Based on AACR2 and MARC 21*, 5th ed. Westport, CT: Libraries Unlimited, 2008.

Additional Information

2

Cataloging-in-Publication

Your first introduction to an authoritative bibliographic record will probably be when you open a book and turn to the back of the title page called a "verso." Most books published today have cataloging-in-publication (CIP, pronounced "sip") information on the verso. National libraries, such as the Library and Archives Canada (LAC), the British Library (BL), and the Library of Congress (LC) (while LC is not a national library, it functions as one in many ways) provide this information. Currently, CIP is an important resource for all types of libraries and media centers, and its use helps to insure that standard cataloging practice is followed in libraries that do not have access to other sources, such as major bibliographic networks. At this writing, however, the program is undergoing reevaluation and reconsideration, and it is not clear what changes may be implemented in the future.

CIP records are created before publication when the items they represent, mainly books, have not yet been finished. As they approach completion, participating publishers send copies of the bibliographic information, such as a book's title page(s) and table of contents, to the appropriate national library, which does as much cataloging as possible from the data in hand. Catalogers at national libraries do not see the actual content of the items they catalog for CIP and must rely on publishers to provide enough information for an accurate CIP record. National library catalogers do all necessary research before assigning the correct bibliographic form of names, appropriate subject headings, and classification numbers. Information, such as the number of pages in books, is left out of the record because it is unknown at the point of CIP cataloging. This CIP record is then sent to the publisher to be printed on the verso. National libraries also enter the CIP records into national bibliographic databases and networks with identifying tags to show that these records are not full or complete.

Catalogers should be aware of the differences in the CIP produced by different national libraries. Sometimes it is the amount of information provided in a CIP record. For example, in Figure 2.1, the CIP prepared by LC for *The Pedant's Revolt* is much more complete than the CIP in Figure 2.2 prepared by BL for *In Search of Genghis Khan*. Sometimes a book will contain two CIPs because the book has been separately published in two countries and the publisher has sent the preliminary materials to two national libraries. Figure 2.3, *Uncle Tungsten*, is an example of this. Note that LC and LAC have made several different cataloging decisions for this book. These decisions will be examined in Chapter 4 about access points, in Chapter 5 about subject headings chosen from the *Library of Congress Subject Headings* list, and in Chapter 6 about classification.

Always look for the source of the CIP record. A few publishers provide a CIP record cataloged by their own staff because they find it less trouble than sending information to their national agency. People unfamiliar with cataloging rules may have done these CIPs,

FIGURE 2.1
(title page)   *(information on verso)*

THE PEDANT'S REVOLT

*Know What
Know-It-Alls Know*

ANDREA BARHAM

DELACORTE PRESS

THE PEDANT'S REVOLT
A Delacorte Book

PUBLISHING HISTORY
Michael O'Mara Press UK hardcover edition published 2005
Delacorte Press hardcover edition / July 2006

Published by
Bantam Dell
A Division of Random House, Inc.
New York, New York

All rights reserved
Copyright © 2005 by Andrea Barham

Book design by Martin Bristow

Delacorte Press is a registered trademark of Random House,
Inc., and the colophon is a trademark of Random House, Inc.

Library of Congress Cataloging in Publication Data
Barham, Andrea.
The pedant's revolt : know what know-it-alls know / Andrea
Barham.
p. cm.
Includes bibliographical references.
ISBN-10: 0-385-34016-8
ISBN-13: 978-0-385-34016-8
1. Common fallacies. I. Title.

AZ999 .B29 2006   2006040159
001.9/6 22

Printed in the United States of America
Published simultaneously in Canada

www.bantamdell.com

10 9 8 7 6 5 4 3 2 1
BVG

and a CIP that has not been cataloged by a national agency should be thoroughly checked. Occasionally, an alternative CIP will be used to make a point. For example, in Figure 2.4, there are two CIPs on the verso of *Radical Cataloging: Essays at the Front*—an LC CIP record and "alternative cataloging-in-publication data." The latter was added to make a point about the content of the book (for example, the editor as main entry as opposed to the title as main entry in the LC CIP).

And also very occasionally, a publisher prints the wrong CIP on the verso of a book as demonstrated in Figure 2.5, where Hammond has put the CIP for its *Citation World Atlas* on the verso of its *Ambassador World Atlas*.

Using CIP to Build a Bibliographic Record

First of all, you must check to be sure that the bibliographic data on the item in hand match the elements given in the CIP record. Sometimes, information in CIP records has to be corrected to reflect changes made by publishers after CIP cataloging has been done. These changes can be as far-reaching as giving a different title to a book or as minor as

FIGURE 2.2
(title page)

Tim Severin

In Search of Genghis Khan

PHOTOGRAPHS BY
PAUL HARRIS

HUTCHINSON
London Sydney Auckland Johannesburg

(information on verso)

© Tim Severin 1991

© Photographs Paul Harris 1991

Plate 1: Portrait of Genghis Khan
© National Palace Museum, Taipei, Taiwan,
Republic of China

Plate 2: Detail from painting by Tchao Pung Fou
© Musée Guimet, Paris/Réunion des Musées Nationaux

We gratefully acknowledge permission to reproduce extracts from
the following:
The Modern History of Mongolia © Kegan Paul International,
London and New York
The History and Life of Chinggis Khan by Onon © E J Brill
The Mission of Friar William of Rubruck 1253–1255 translated
by P Jackson with D Morgan © Hakluyt Society
The Travels of Marco Polo translated by Ronald Latham,
Penguin Classics © Ronald Latham 1958

The right of Tim Severin to be identified as
Author of this work has been asserted by
Tim Severin in accordance with the Copy-
right, Designs and Patents Act, 1988

This edition first published in 1991 by Hutchinson

Random Century Group Ltd
20 Vauxhall Bridge Road, London SW1V 2SA

Random Century Australia Ltd
20 Alfred Street, Milsons Point, Sydney,
NSW 2061, Australia

Random Century New Zealand Ltd
PO Box 40, 086, Glenfield, Auckland 10, New Zealand

Random Century South Africa Ltd
PO Box 337, Berglvei, 2012, South Africa

British Library Cataloguing-in-Publication Data
Severin, Tim
In search of Genghis Khan.
I. Title
915.1704

ISBN 0-09-174779-1

Colour repro by Colorlito, Milan
Typeset by 🅰 Tek Art Ltd, Addiscombe, Croydon, Surrey
Printed and bound in Great Britain by
Butler and Tanner Ltd, Frome, Somerset

---

adding a foreword or a frontispiece. Occasionally, a totally incorrect CIP appears on the verso. Catalogers should be particularly careful in checking the CIP of older books that are being added to the collection because rules for descriptive cataloging, subject heading terms, and classification numbers may have changed since the books were published. Despite these discrepancies, to which good catalogers must be alert, CIP is usually reliable, trustworthy work, performed carefully and thoroughly by some of the best catalogers in each nation.

FIGURE 2.3
(title page)

UNCLE TUNGSTEN

Memories of a Chemical Boyhood

OLIVER SACKS

ALFRED A. KNOPF
NEW YORK · TORONTO
2001

(information on verso)

THIS IS A BORZOI BOOK
PUBLISHED BY ALFRED A. KNOPF
AND ALFRED A. KNOPF CANADA

Copyright © 2001 by Oliver Sacks

All rights reserved under International and Pan-American Copyright Conventions. Published in the United States by Alfred A. Knopf, a division of Random House, Inc., New York, and distributed by Random House, Inc., New York. Published simultaneously in Canada by Alfred A. Knopf Canada, a division of Random House of Canada Limited, Toronto, and distributed by Random House of Canada Limited, Toronto.

www.aaknopf.com
www.randomhouse.ca
www.oliversacks.com

Knopf, Borzoi Books, and the colophon are registered trademarks of Random House, Inc.

Library of Congress Cataloging-in-Publication Data
Sacks, Oliver W.
Uncle Tungsten : memories of a chemical boyhood /
Oliver Sacks. — 1st ed.
p.   cm.
ISBN 0-375-40448-1
1. Sacks, Oliver W.   2. Neurologists—England—Biography.
I. Title
RC339.52.S23 A3 2001
616.8'092—dc21
[B]   2001033738

National Library of Canada Cataloguing in Publication Data
Sacks, Oliver, 1933–
Uncle Tungsten: memories of a chemical boyhood
ISBN 0-676-97261-6
1. Sacks, Oliver, 1933–   —Childhood and youth.
2. Sacks, Oliver, 1933–   —Knowledge—Chemistry.   I. Title.
QD22.S23A3 2001   540'.92   C2001-930571-0

Manufactured in the United States of America
First Edition

The work done by national library catalogers in establishing call numbers, name headings, and subject descriptors can be used by local librarians and media specialists to select headings, determine titles proper, assign call numbers, and complete accurate bibliographic descriptions.

Local libraries vary in their use of CIP records depending on the agency's need for accuracy and the availability of alternative information sources, as well as the expertise of the cataloging staff in improving the CIP records. Local libraries can decide to:

- accept and use CIP records as given;

- use CIP after checking the items in hand and making corrections when necessary;

- ignore CIP, generally because other sources of bibliographic information are available.

The first decision—accept and use CIP records as given—is the cheapest method, but also the one that produces a less reliable catalog. The second decision—checking the items

FIGURE 2.4
(title page)

Radical Cataloging

(information on verso)

Essays at the Front

edited by K. R. Roberto

INTRODUCTION BY SANFORD BERMAN

ALSO OF INTEREST

Revolting Librarians Redux:
Radical Librarians Speak Out,
by K. R. Roberto and Jessamyn West
(McFarland, 2003)

ALTERNATIVE CATALOGING-IN-PUBLICATION DATA

Roberto, K. R. (Keller R.), 1975–, editor.
Radical cataloging: essays at the front. Edited by K.R. Roberto.
Introduction by Sanford Berman.— Jefferson, North Carolina:
McFarland & Company, Inc., Publishers, copyright 2008.

Includes criticisms of traditional Library of Congress cataloging
and subject headings, discussion of how cataloging practices affect
front-line library workers, and suggestions for methods to make
cataloging more inclusive and helpful to library users.

PARTIAL CONTENTS: 1. Cataloging in context —
2. We criticize because we care — 3. Innovative practices.
1. Critical cataloging.   2. Catalogers — Social responsibility.
3. Library of Congress cataloging.   4. Cataloging — Anecdotes.
I. Title: Rad cataloging.   II. Title: Essays at the front.   III. Title: Frontline essays.
Z693 .R63 2008

LIBRARY OF CONGRESS CATALOGUING-IN-PUBLICATION DATA

Radical cataloging : essays at the front / edited by K. R. Roberto ;
introduction by Sanford Berman.
p.   cm.
Includes bibliographical references and index.

ISBN 978-0-7864-3543-2
softcover : 50# alkaline paper ∞

1. Cataloging.   I. Roberto, K. R. (Keller R.), 1975–
Z693.R33   2008   025.3 — dc22   2008007084

British Library cataloguing data are available

©2008 K. R. Roberto. All rights reserved

No part of this book may be reproduced or transmitted in any form
or by any means, electronic or mechanical, including photocopying
or recording, or by any information storage and retrieval system,
without permission in writing from the publisher.

Cover photograph ©2007 Shutterstock

Manufactured in the United States of America

McFarland & Company, Inc., Publishers
Box 611, Jefferson, North Carolina 28640
www.mcfarlandpub.com

McFarland & Company, Inc., Publishers
Jefferson, North Carolina, and London

in hand and making necessary corrections to the CIP information—results in a more accurate catalog. If a complete and accurate bibliographic record is available from a recognized source, the third decision might be the best choice.

FIGURE 2.5
(title page)   *(information on verso)*

HAMMOND

Ambassador World Atlas

HAMMOND World Atlas
Part of the Langenscheidt Publishing Group   **L**

Hammond Publications Advisory Board

Library of Congress Cataloging-In-Publication Data
Hammond World Atlas Corporation.
    Citation world atlas. -- Rev.
        p.   cm.
    At head of title: Hammond
    Includes indexes.
    ISBN 0-8437-1295-3 (softcover)
    ISBN 0-8437-1382-8 (hardcover)
    1. Atlases. I. Title. II. Title: Hammond citiation world atlas.
G1021. H2446   1998   <G&M>
912--DC21   98-12358
                                           CIP
                                           MAP

Looking at a CIP in Detail

Turn to the CIP data in Figure 2.1 on page 6 for *The Pedant's Revolt*. The following is a quick review of the meaning of each line. Details about each part of the bibliographic record will be discussed in more detail later in this book.

First line: "Barham, Andrea."—bibliographic form of the author's name.

Second line contains area 1 information (title and responsibility for the intellectual content of the work): "The pedant's revolt : know what know-it-alls know / Andrea Barham"— the title (called "title proper"), the subtitle (called "other title information"), and the author's name (called "statement of responsibility") with internationally accepted capitalization and punctuation.

Third line contains area 5 (physical description information): "p. cm." Because at the time the publisher submitted the bibliographic information to the national library, the number and type of paging and the size of the book were incomplete or unknown, many CIPs do not include this line. (Note that the LAC CIP in Figure 2.3 on page 8 does not.)

Fourth line contains area 7 (notes information): "includes bibliographical references"— various miscellaneous information that is not mandated in other areas can be added to this note area.

Fifth and sixth lines contain area 8 (standard numbers and terms of availability information): International Standard Book Numbers (ISBN).

Seventh line: "tracing," which in this case includes an LC subject heading and a direction to make a title added entry.

Eighth line: "AZ999.B29 2006" is the LC classification number; "2006040159" is the LC control number. (Note that in Figure 2.3 on page 8, "C2001-930571-0" is the LAC control number).

Ninth line: "001.9/6" is the Dewey decimal classification number; "/" is a prime mark described on page 97; "22" indicates that this number was found in the 22nd edition of the *Dewey Decimal Classification and Relative Index*, which is often indicated in the following manner: "001.0/6—dc22."

Subject headings and classification numbers that have been taken from other lists and schemes, such as those published by the National Library of Medicine for specialized health science libraries, are placed in square brackets. General libraries can ignore these because they do not need greater specificity in classification and subject headings for their collections. Brackets also enclose headings from LC's annotated card program for children's materials (see Figure 5.8 on page 78).

How we make use of this information to create a complete bibliographic record will be discussed in the next five chapters.

International Standard Bibliographic Description

The acronym "ISBD" is used in this book. It stands for International Standard Bibliographic Description, which was developed by the International Federation of Library Associations and Institutions (IFLA) to facilitate global uniformity in bibliographic records and enable libraries to use records from other jurisdictions. The ISBD order of bibliographic elements and the ISBD's prescribed punctuation are found in the next chapter, which discusses descriptive cataloging.

Additional Information

3

Descriptive Cataloging

Describing an item usually is the first activity catalogers perform. This involves recording information from the item that identifies it uniquely and completely, differentiating it from similar items with which it might be confused. Chapter 4 completes this part of the cataloging process for books by explaining and illustrating the selection of access points and the way in which they are derived from descriptive elements.

Anglo-American Cataloguing Rules

Current at this writing, the standard code of rules for description and access used by North American libraries is *Anglo-American Cataloguing Rules*, second edition, 2002 revision, and its updates ending in 2005 (AACR2-2005). AACR2-2005 is used beyond the shores of North America in the United Kingdom, Australia, New Zealand, and other English-speaking countries. A number of authorized translations enable it to be used also by catalogers in countries outside the English-speaking world. AACR2-2005 is available in two formats: in a printed edition and online as part of a product called *Cataloger's Desktop*.

AACR2-2005 is divided into two parts, Part I covering descriptive cataloging and Part II covering access points. In addition, five appendixes instruct about proper capitalization (Appendix A), abbreviation (Appendix B), and numerals (Appendix C), furnish a glossary (Appendix D), and list initial articles in multiple languages (Appendix E). A comprehensive index completes the text. In Part I, chapters after the first are organized by physical medium. Because we are learning to catalog books, in Part I we shall be concerned only with the first chapter, which covers general rules applicable to all materials regardless of the physical form in which they appear, and Chapter 2 devoted to books. The first chapter also contains a few special rules for materials consisting of parts in multiple formats and materials that are reproductions of other materials. The cataloging of such materials is usually done by experienced catalogers and need not be considered here.

Level of Description

AACR2 offers three choices for description:

Level 1 is the simplest and least detailed level, and is considered appropriate for libraries with small collections serving people doing uncomplicated searches. Level 1 descriptions for books do not include (a) information that appears in the primary/main heading about the single author of a work; (b) subtitles; (c) places of publication; (d) series titles; (e) statements of responsibility for editions; and (f) only require the extent of an item to be given (for example, the number of pages in a book, but not the presence of illustrations or the book's dimensions). However, libraries can add information normally omitted from a level 1 record if that piece of information is considered useful for their catalog users. This is called enhanced level 1.

Level 2 is a middle-ground level that includes more detail than level 1. It is the standard level of description selected by national libraries and bibliographic networks for "full level" cataloging. Level 2 descriptions are considered sufficient to serve the needs of scholarly researchers using large collections of materials. In addition to all the information that is part of a level 1 record, level 2 requires the inclusion of subtitles and other title information, statements of responsibility, place(s) of publication, the presence of illustrations, the dimensions of a book, and series statements. This level of detail helps to distinguish different works with similar titles and different editions of the same title and facilitates the selection of items with specific characteristics desired by searchers.

Level 3 is the most detailed level. It requires the inclusion of every detail mandated by the rules that are applicable to the items being cataloged. Level 3 descriptions are, by definition, the most detailed work possible. Such work is likely to be desired primarily for special collections serving the needs of specialized clients. Because beginning catalogers are unlikely to handle such materials, level 3 cataloging is not discussed in this book.

Number and Order of Bibliographic Elements

The number of descriptive elements, called "areas of description," and their order in catalog records also has evolved over the centuries. ISBD mandates eight areas of description, although all eight are not required for every material format. The ISBD model is as follows:

Area 1:   Title and statement(s) of responsibility (also called title statement)
Area 2:   Edition statement
Area 3:   Material specific details (not used for books)
Area 4:   Publication, distribution information
Area 5:   Physical description
Area 6:   Series statement
Area 7:   Notes (optional for books)
Area 8:   Standard numbers (ISBN for books) and terms of availability

Identifying Punctuation

ISBD punctuation identifies each element and subelement of description in a manner used by early computer programmers. It was developed to facilitate programming as well as handle bibliographic information in unfamiliar languages and scripts. Although current programming methods probably do not rely on it anymore, ISBD punctuation has persisted and can be helpful to catalogers and/or acquisitions librarians when they retrieve records in languages and scripts they cannot read.

The ISBD model is the "glue" that knits national or local variations in descriptive cataloging into packages of data consistent enough to be merged and manipulated in commonly held databases. ISBD punctuation requires that a full stop (a period), a space, a dash, and another space precede the beginning of each area of description to separate it from the beginning of the previous area, unless that area begins in a new paragraph. In North American tradition, card-style catalog records placed areas 1 through 4 together in one paragraph, areas 5 and 6 in the next paragraph, each note in a new paragraph, and

FIGURE 3.1

```
This example is an illustration of:
    • fiction book
    • publishing date not listed; copyright date given
    • no illustrations
    • title added entry
    • National Library of Canada (i.e., Library and Archives of
      Canada) CIP
```

1st level cataloging

```
Barfoot, Joan.
  Critical injuries. -- Key Porter, c2001.
  336 p.

  ISBN 1-55263-347-0.
```

2nd level cataloging

```
Barfoot, Joan.
  Critical injuries / Joan Barfoot. -- Toronto : Key Porter,
c2001.
  336 p. ; 23 cm.

  ISBN 1-55263-347-0.
```

Fig. 3.1—Continues

area 8 in its own paragraph. As a result, the full stop-space-dash-space was used to separate areas 1 and 2, 2 and 3 if it is used, and 3 and 4. Because area 3 is not used in book cataloging, the punctuation would appear between areas 1, 2, and 4 and between areas 5 and 6. It is important to realize that ISBD punctuation precedes an element in the description rather than follows it, as is customary in written English. In other words, punctuation alerts the catalog user to the type of information that follows the punctuation.

Sources of Information

Each physical format has several information sources, one of which is considered the best, or "chief," source. For books and other printed materials, the chief source is the title page, including its verso. Other places (called "prescribed sources") recommended by the rules include the "preliminaries" (the cover and all the pages up to the title page verso); colophon (the last page, if it contains bibliographic information, but not if it is merely the final page of the text, appendix, index, etc.; the colophon is more usually found in books published outside of North America); the rest of the book; and accompanying material issued with the book by the publisher. In Figures 3.1 and 3.2 on pages 15–18, no major differences appear in the way titles, authors, etc., are presented; but, in some books, titles, names, dates, and other elements are dramatically different, depending on where one looks.

FIGURE 3.1 *(continued)*

(title page)

Critical Injuries

Joan Barfoot

(information on verso)

National Library of Canada Cataloguing in Publication Data

Barfoot, Joan, 1946–
    Critical injuries

ISBN 1-55263-347-0

I. Title

PS8553.A7624C74 2001   C813'.54   C2001-900981-X
PR9199.3.B37C74 2001

The publisher gratefully acknowledges the support of the Canada Council for the Arts and the Ontario Arts Council for its publishing program.

We acknowledge the financial support of the Government of Canada through the Book Publishing Industry Development Program (BDIPD) for our publishing activities.

Key Porter Books Limited
70 The Esplanade
Toronto, Ontario
Canada M5E 1R2
www.keyporter.com

Electronic formatting: Heidi Palfrey
Design: Peter Maher

Printed and bound in Canada

01 02 03 04 05 06 6 5 4 3 2 1

KEY PORTER BOOKS

Area 1: Title and Statements of Responsibility

The first piece of information in a bibliographic description is the title statement, which, for books, generally consists of three elements (see Figure 3.1):

FIGURE 3.2

This example is an illustration of:
- three dots in title replaced by long dash to avoid confusion with marks of omission
- other title information (in 2nd level cataloging)
- detailed pagination
- bibliography and index note (in 2nd level cataloging)
- two ISBNs listed on verso, only one noted in the bibliographic record
- ISBN qualified
- Library of Congress CIP
- two levels of cataloging

1st level cataloging

```
Neiburger, Eli.
  Gamers — in the library?! -- American Library Association, 2007.
  ix, 178 p.

  ISBN-13: 978-0-8389-0944-7 (alk. paper).
```

2nd level cataloging

```
Neiburger, Eli.
  Gamers — in the library?! : the why, what, and how of videogame
tournaments for all ages / Eli Neiburger. -- Chicago : American Library
Association, 2007.
  ix, 178 p. : ill. ; 23 cm.

  Includes bibliographical references and index.
  ISBN-13: 978-0-8389-0944-7 (alk. paper).
```

Fig. 3.2—Continues

- The main title (called the "title proper").

- Other title words or phrases, such as subtitles (called "other title information" in AACR2-2005). With a few exceptions, all title words appearing between the end of the main title and the beginning of the statement of responsibility are considered "other title information." The principal exceptions are parallel titles, which are the main titles translated into other languages or scripts, and alternative titles, which are titles preceded by the word "or" that follow the main titles, for example, *Trial by Jury, or, The Lass Who Loved a Sailor*. Parallel titles are separated from the main title by a space-equal sign-space. Alternative titles are considered integral parts of the main titles.

- Statement(s) of responsibility.

The only prescribed source for the title statement is the chief source, that is, the title page. In Figure 3.1, there is no other title information, so only the title proper and the

FIGURE 3.2 *(continued)*

(title page)

Gamers . . . in the Library?!
The Why, What, and How
of Videogame Tournaments
for All Ages

Eli Neiburger

(information on verso)

The paper used in this publication meets the minimum requirements of American National Standard for Information Sciences—Permanence of Paper for Printed Library Materials, ANSI Z39.48-1992. ♾

Library of Congress Cataloging-in-Publication Data
Neiburger, Eli.
     Gamers . . . in the library?! : the why, what, and how of videogame
tournaments for all ages / Eli Neiburger.
         p.   cm.
     Includes bibliographical references and index.
     ISBN-13: 978-0-8389-0944-7 (alk. paper)
     1. Video games. 2. Computer games. 3. Libraries and teenagers—United
States.   I. Title.
GV1469.3.N45 2007
794.8—dc22   2007010512

ISBN-13: 978-0-8389-0944-7
ISBN-10: 0-8389-0944-2

Printed in the United States of America
11 10 09 08 07   5 4 3 2 1

AMERICAN LIBRARY ASSOCIATION
Chicago   2007

author are given in area 1. If the title is taken from another source, the source must be stated in the note area. The words of the title statement are copied from the item being cataloged exactly as they appear there, except for the way they are capitalized and punctuated.

Capitalization follows the rules given in AACR2-2005's Appendix A, which for English-language titles says to capitalize the first word of the main title and proper nouns, but no others. The punctuation is altered to avoid the use of colons, semicolons, equal signs, square brackets, or slashes, and other cataloging conventions. For example, in Figure 3.2, the three dots in the title have been replaced by a long dash (—) so that these dots are not confused with AACR2-2005's convention of three dots to indicate marks of omission.

Marks of omission can be used to shorten any part of a long title after the first five words of that title. Marks of omission are also found in statements of responsibility when there are more than three principal authors (see Figure 4.2 on page 39).

FIGURE 3.3

```
This example is an illustration of:
    • primary statement of responsibility as part of the title
      proper
    • detailed pagination
    • numbered series statement (in 2nd level cataloging)
    • contents note (in 2nd level cataloging)
```

1st level cataloging

```
Aristotle.
  Aristotle's politics and poetics. -- Viking, 1957.
  xvi, 265 p.
```

2nd level cataloging

```
Aristotle.
  Aristotle's politics and poetics / translated by Benjamin Jowett &
Thomas Twining ; with an introduction by Lincoln Diamant. -- New York :
Viking, 1957.
  xvi, 265 p. ; 20 cm. -- (Compass books, 20)

  Contents: Politics / translated by Benjamin Jowett -- Poetics /
translated by Thomas Twining.
```

Fig. 3.3—Continues

In Figure 3.2, because punctuation is part of the title, it must be included in the title statement. Figure 3.2 also has other title information that is given following the title proper. If any other sources on the item—covers, spines, versos, colophons, captions, credits, labels, boxes, etc.—bear different titles, they are transcribed also, but not in the title statement (see Area 7: Notes on page 27).

Statements of responsibility are given exactly as they appear on the chief source of information. If the statement of responsibility is taken from another source, the statement is enclosed in square brackets. Some parts of personal names that establish an author's qualifications for writing the book found on a title page are omitted, such as academic degrees, places of work, etc. Words, such as "editor" or "compiled," are not abbreviated in this area.

If the name of the person responsible for the intellectual content of a work forms part of the title and is not listed in a statement of responsibility on the title page, the name is not repeated in the statement of responsibility (see Figure 3.3).

ISBD Punctuation for area 1:
- Other title information (subtitle) is preceded by a space-colon-space.

- The statement of responsibility is preceded by a space-slash-space.

- The statement of subsidiary responsibility is preceded by a space-semicolon-space.

FIGURE 3.3 *(continued)*

(cover)

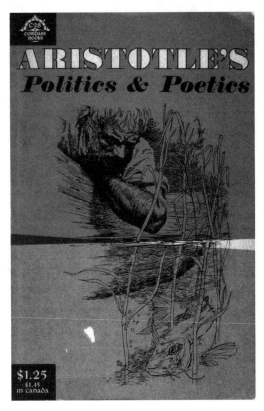

Fig. 3.3—Continues

Example: *John's rolling ball : a tale of adventure* / by Priscilla Brown ; illustrated by Mary Green.

First level description includes title proper and statement of responsibility; however, if the statement of responsibility is identical to the information contained in the main entry, it is not given.

Area 2: Edition Statements

If an edition or an equivalent statement is named on the item, it is transcribed exactly as it appears on the item, after the title and statement(s) of responsibility area. Words in the edition statement may be abbreviated if they appear that way on the item or if abbreviations for them appear in AACR2-2005 Appendixes B and C. For example, if a given title page says "Third Edition," it would be transcribed into the description as "3rd ed." Below is a table of edition statements one might see on the title pages or versos of books and the way they would be given in the bibliographic descriptions:

FIGURE 3.3 *(continued)*

(information on verso)

COMPASS BOOKS EDITION
ISSUED 1957 BY THE VIKING PRESS

SECOND PRINTING APRIL 1959
THIRD PRINTING JULY 1960

(title page)

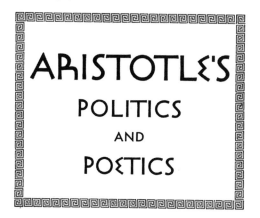

ARISTOTLE'S
POLITICS
AND
POETICS

Translated by
BENJAMIN JOWETT & THOMAS TWINING
with an Introduction by
LINCOLN DIAMANT

New York: The Viking Press

DISTRIBUTED IN CANADA BY
THE MACMILLAN COMPANY OF CANADA LIMITED

THIS EDITION PUBLISHED BY ARRANGEMENT WITH THE
WORLD PUBLISHING COMPANY. SPECIAL CONTENTS COPY-
RIGHT 1952 BY THE WORLD PUBLISHING COMPANY.

PRINTED IN U.S.A. BY THE COLONIAL PRESS INC.

WORDS ON ITEM	TRANSCRIPTION
First revised edition	1st rev. ed.
First edition, revised & enlarged	1st ed., rev. & enl.
Édition française	Éd. française
Fourth Edition Completely Revised	4th ed. completely rev.
Large Print Edition	Large print ed.
Second abridged edition	2nd abridged ed.

Sometimes, the CIP lists an edition statement that is not found elsewhere in the book. For example, in Figure 2.3 on page 8, the LC CIP lists an edition statement "1st ed." and the LAC CIP does not. Because "1st edition" is not found elsewhere in the book, the bibliographic record should not list an edition statement.

ISBD punctuation for area 2: If a book is edited or revised by a person other than the author, the responsibility statement is preceded by a space-slash-space, for example, 4th ed. / revised by Jane Brown. (Note that "revised" in a statement of responsibility is not abbreviated.)

First level description includes solely the edition statement transcribed as it appears on the material using the appropriate transcription. Although an edition statement is mandated for first level cataloging, it is common practice that first editions are not given even though they are noted in the book. However, when a first edition statement distinguishes a publication in an important way, it is included in a first level description. For example, in Figure 4.2 on page 39, the edition statement distinguishes the Canadian edition from the U.S. edition of this book.

Area 4: Publication, Distribution Information

This area generally consists of three parts: (1) the place of publication, usually a city; (2) the name of the publisher; and (3) the date of publication. Information given in area 4 is transcribed from the item being cataloged as succinctly as possible, which means giving, usually, only the first place of publication, the publisher's name, and the year of publication. Catalogers are allowed to abbreviate some location information (states and provinces, for example) and abridge names when this can be done without creating confusion.

When information in the book states that it is distributed by a firm other than the publisher, information about the distributor is also given. (See Figure 3.5 on page 27.) More than one place of publication and the publisher's or distributor's name may be given for specific reasons, for example, when the first named place and/or the publisher is in a country foreign to the cataloging institution and an additional place and/or publisher is located in the home country, or when another place/publisher appears more prominently than the first named. In both those instances, two places/names are given. Figure 4.9 on page 55 is an example of a book published in two countries, the United States and England. Note the difference in the publication, distribution information that is given for the book when it is housed in an American library and when it is housed in a Canadian library. On the other hand, look at the title page for Figure 2.2 on page 7, where four places of publication are listed on the title page. Catalogers in the United States and Canada would give only "London" as the place of publication.

Dates of publication are so important that catalogers are not permitted to leave them out of catalog records. Under earlier cataloging rules, if catalogers did not find a date, they were allowed to enter "[n.d.]" ("no date") in the record. This practice was abolished when AACR2 was published in 1978.

Many publications list more than one date. If this is the case, choose the date to be given in the bibliographic record in the following order:

FIGURE 3.4

This example is an illustration of:
- fuller form of name in main access point (in 2nd level cataloging)
- multiple dates on verso
- series statement (in 2nd level cataloging)
- edition and history note (in 2nd level cataloging)
- two levels of cataloging

1st level cataloging

```
Forster, E.M.
  A passage to India. -- Penguin Books, 1961.
  316 p.
```

2nd level cataloging

```
Forster, E.M. (Edward Morgan).
  A passage to India / E.M. Forster. -- Middlesex, England : Penguin
Books, 1961.
  316 p. ; 18 cm. -- (Penguin modern classics)

  First published by Edward Arnold in 1924.
```

Fig. 3.4—Continues

(1) Date of publication for the item in hand, for example, 2008.

(2) Latest copyright date, for example, c2008.

(3) Printing date, for example, 2008 printing.

    Figure 3.4 is an example of many dates listed on a verso. The book was first published in 1924 and has been reissued many times in three formats. The fact that it has a single copyright date (1924) suggests that no changes have occurred in the text of the book. Therefore, the date in the catalog record for this format of the book (Penguin Modern Classics) would be 1961, not the latest reprinting date. A note should also be made to indicate that this book retains the same text as the 1924 publication.

    When no date at all is given on the item and it cannot be found anywhere (order records and reference sources are the best places to look for them), catalogers must give their best guess as to the year the item was published. Depending on the probability that the guess is accurate, catalogers may add question marks to their guessed date, for example, [2007?], give alternate years, for example, [2003 or 2004], suggest spans of years, for example, [1998–2002?], or use question marks in place of digits indicating a decade, for example, [197–?] or a century, for example, [19–?]. All of the guessed dates are enclosed within square brackets, because they did not come from the prescribed sources. Figure 4.8 on page 53 is an example of a guessed date. In this case, the thirteen-digit ISBN gives a clue that the book could not have been published before 2007, the date that

FIGURE 3.4 *(continued)*

(title page)	*(information on verso)*

(title page)

E. M. FORSTER

A Passage to India

PENGUIN BOOKS

(information on verso)

Penguin Books Ltd, Harmondsworth, Middlesex, England
Penguin Books Pty Ltd, Ringwood, Victoria, Australia

First published by Edward Arnold 1924
Published in Penguin Books 1936
Reprinted 1936, 1937 (twice),
1939, 1940, 1941, 1943, 1950, 1952, 1954, 1957, 1959, 1960
Reissued in Penguin Modern Classics 1961
Reprinted 1962, 1963, 1964, 1965, 1966

Copyright © E. M. Forster, 1924

Made and printed in Great Britain
by Hazell Watson & Viney Ltd,
Aylesbury, Bucks
Set in Monotype Garamond

the thirteen-digit ISBN was inaugurated. The book was received in the library in 2008, so that date of publication has to be either 2007 or 2008, therefore, [2007 or 2008] is the correct recording of the date.

Sometimes, libraries receive unpublished items, such as local histories, reports of meetings, etc. Such unpublished items do not have "publication" dates. Instead, the date of an unpublished item's creation is given in area 4, but no place of publication or publisher can be included.

If no place of publication is listed on a book, "[S.l.]" meaning "sine loco" (no place) is given in the catalog record. Similarly, "[s.n.]" meaning "sine nomine" (no name) is used in the absence of a publisher's name. It is reported that *RDA: Resource Description and Access* (see page 31) will replace "[S.l.]" with "place not recorded" or "place not known" and [s.n.] with "publisher not recorded" or "publisher not known."

ISBD punctuation for area 4:

- Publisher is preceded by a space-colon-space.

- Date is preceded by a simple comma with no preceding space.

- Distributor statement is preceded by a space-semicolon-space.

Example: London : Gifford, 2006 ; New York : Firefly [distributor], 2008.

First level description includes the name of the first publisher or distributor and the date of publication or distribution.

Area 5: Physical Description

Information in this area consists of four parts:

(1) The extent of an item—books are described in terms of preliminary pages, pages of text, leaves (pages printed on only one side), or volumes, as appropriate.

(2) Other physical details—illustrations; optionally, the type of illustrations can be listed. AACR2-2005 lists the following types to be noted (allowed abbreviations are in parentheses): coats of arms, facsimiles (facsim(s).), forms, genealogical table(s) (geneal. table(s)), maps, music, plans, portraits (port(s).), samples.

(3) Dimensions—the height of the spines; only when the width of a book is greater than the height of a book are both dimensions given. See Exercise 5D on page 84.

(4) Accompanying materials, if any, issued with the material being cataloged—discs, maps, tapes, photographs, or other materials placed in pockets inside the front or back covers. Note that a map reproduced on one of the pages of a book or on endpapers is recorded in the illustration statement, but a map placed in a pocket inside the cover that can be removed from the book is considered accompanying material.

ISBD punctuation for area 5:

- Commas plus one space, but with no preceding space, separate various types of paging in the extent of item.

- The illustration statement is preceded by a space-colon-space, and commas with no preceding space separate various types of illustrations.

- Space-semicolon-space precedes the dimensions.

- Space-plus sign-space precedes accompanying materials.

Examples:

xii, 298 p. : ill. ; 28 cm.	(book with preliminary pages and general illustrations)
2 v. : ill. ; 29 cm. + 3 maps	(work in more than one volume with separate maps in a pocket inside the back cover)
[132] leaves ; 20 cm.	(all unpaged leaves, no illustrations)
65 p. : all col. ill. ; 32 cm.	(colored picture book without text)
78 p. : chiefly col. ill. ; 32 cm.	(colored picture book with text)
396 p. : ill., maps, ports ; 27 cm.	(illustrations specified)
105 p. : ill., ports. ; 21 x 26 cm.	(book's width is greater than height)

First level description includes only the number and type of pages.

Area 6: Series Statement

Series statements are recorded in this area of description when they appear on an item. Usually the series statement is found in one place in a book. However, in some instances, the series can be stated differently on the same item. For example, in Figure 3.5, the series statement is found on the front cover as "CBC Massey Lectures," on the back cover as "CBC Massey Lectures Series," and on the page preceding the title page as "The Massey Lectures Series." The CIP on the verso lists "CBC Massey lecture series." Is this a spelling mistake (lecture/lectures)? The cataloger will need to do some research to ascertain what the library has previously called this series, and, if this is the first book in this series in the library's collection, what series statement was used in this series' previous publications.

Publishers and distributors of materials sometimes put statements on the versos of title pages that seem to be series statements, but are not. Such statements may even use the word "series." A rule of thumb for determining whether a title is a genuine series title is to ask if it appears as part of a full sentence, such as "This book is one of a series of scholarly works emanating from the University College annual lectures." If the answer to the question is "yes," the statement is not a series title, but an explanation of the origin of the contents. A real series title would be worded more like an ordinary title and capitalized accordingly, for example, "University College Annual Lectures."

If there is a number accompanying the series statement, this number is also recorded. (see Figure 3.3 on page 19). If there are two or more series with the same title, statements of responsibility may also be given. Sometimes, International Standard Serial Numbers (ISSNs) are assigned to series titles and may also be recorded in this area. Beginning catalogers are unlikely to deal with these types of materials.

ISBD punctuation for area 6:

- The area is enclosed in parentheses.

- The numbering within a series is preceded by a space-semicolon-space.

- See AACR2-2005 rule 2.6A1 for the punctuation of complicated series statements.

Examples: (Library and information science text series)

(CLIR publication ; no. 141)

FIGURE 3.5

This example is an illustration of:
- distributor noted (in 2nd level cataloging)
- publication date not listed, copyright date given
- series statement (in 2nd level cataloging)
- index note (in 2nd level cataloging)
- two ISBNs listed on back cover, only one noted in the bibliographic record
- ISBN qualified
- series added entry (in 2nd level cataloging)
- Library and Archives of Canada CIP
- two levels of cataloging

1st level cataloging

```
Manguel, Alberto.
  The city of words. -- Anansi, c2007.
  166 p.

  ISBN-13: 978-0-88784-763-9 (pbk).
```

2nd level cataloging

```
Manguel, Alberto.
  The city of words / Alberto Manguel. -- Toronto : Anansi :
distributed by Harper Collins, c2007.
  166 p. ; 21 cm. -- (CBC Massey lectures series)

  Includes index.
  ISBN-13: 978-0-88784-763-9 (pbk).
```

Fig. 3.5—Continues

First level bibliographic description. Series information is omitted. However, if a series title would be a useful access point in the catalog, it must be included here as the basis for the access point (series titles are a type of added entry heading, explained further in Chapter 4). For example, a teacher finds a useful title in a series and wants to see if the series has other titles he or she could use; or, a young reader likes one or two titles in a series and wants to read more; or, a collection-development librarian wants to add to the library's collection all the titles in a scholarly series.

Area 7: Notes

The seventh area of description is devoted to information that users of the catalog might find helpful but does not belong in any of the previous areas. Although notes for books are optional, in some instances, the added information in notes is crucial for selecting

FIGURE 3.5 *(continued)*

(information on cover)

Fig. 3.5—Continues

an edition or version of a title that meets specific user needs, for example, knowing that a work is indexed or has a bibliography, or that it is a sequel to another work, or is a prize-winning book. Catalog searchers who, for any reason, cannot examine materials directly rely on note information to explain enough about the materials to decide if obtaining them is worthwhile. Therefore, notes should be made with as much attention, care, and accuracy as the other areas of description. A selection of important notes related to books are described and illustrated in the following paragraphs:

- Contents note: Here is the place where the titles of individual works in anthologies are given. It is particularly important if library users are more likely to search for the individual works than for the titles of the anthologies in which they are published. Few searchers ask for titles such as *Three Plays by Ibsen* or *The Great Novels of Thomas Hardy*. They usually are looking for one of the plays or novels and want to know whether it is in a particular anthology. Added entries for the titles of the individual works cannot be made unless the reason for them appears in the catalog record. This note is where the reason can be found (see Figure 3.3 on page 19 and Figure 4.9 on page 55).

FIGURE 3.5 *(continued)*

(title page)

The City
of Words

Alberto Manguel

ANANSI

(information on verso)

Published in 2007 by
House of Anansi Press Inc.
110 Spadina Avenue, Suite 801
Toronto, ON, M5V 2K4
Tel. 416-363-4343
Fax 416-363-1017
www.anansi.ca

Distributed in Canada by
HarperCollins Canada Ltd.
1995 Markham Road
Scarborough, ON, M1B 5M8
Toll free tel. 1-800-387-0117

11 10 09 08 07   1 2 3 4 5

LIBRARY AND ARCHIVES CANADA CATALOGUING IN PUBLICATION DATA

Manguel, Alberto, 1948–
The city of words / Alberto Manguel.

(CBC Massey lecture series)
Includes index.
ISBN 978-0-88784-763-9

1. Toleration. 2. Violence. 3. Literature and society.
4. Fiction — Social aspects. I. Title. II. Series.

HM1271.M356 2007   303.6   C2007-903437-3

Library of Congress Control Number: 2007928058

Cover design: Bill Douglas
Typesetting: Laura Brady, Brady Typesetting & Design

Canada Council   Conseil des Arts
for the Arts   du Canada

ONTARIO ARTS COUNCIL
CONSEIL DES ARTS DE L'ONTARIO

We acknowledge for their financial support of our publishing program the Canada Council for the Arts, the Ontario Arts Council, and the Government of Canada through the Book Publishing Industry Development Program (BPIDP).

Printed and bound in Canada

• Summary note: In the past, summary notes were considered an unnecessary part of a catalog record because patrons could go to library shelves to examine items directly and decide on the spot if they wanted to borrow them. For many years, summary notes were added only to records for children's materials (see Figure 5.7 on page 76), but not the rest of the collection. In the twenty-first century, however, many people search catalogs on the World Wide Web from their homes or offices and ask for materials to be put on reserve for pickup or sent to them via interlibrary loans or electronic transmission. Therefore, summary notes have become an important addition to catalog records for all materials. Summary notes should be brief and objective but thorough in covering the content of the materials. Beginning catalogers are unlikely to provide a summary note that is not found in a CIP record.

Rather than add contents notes or summaries, some libraries provide a link to a book's table of contents or to a description of the contents on a publisher's Web site.

- Details of the library's copy note: This is the appropriate place to describe unique characteristics of the holding library's copy that do not appear in any other copies issued by the publisher or distributor, such as special markings, torn or missing pages, autographs, margin notes, etc.

- Numbers on the item note: Although the final area of description is the proper place to include the ISBN of an item, other important numbers may appear on materials that should be given in the catalog record. This note is where all but the ISBN can be given, including Library of Congress Control Numbers (LCCNs), product code numbers, publishers' catalog numbers, etc. Some of the numbers are encoded in specially designated fields when catalog records are entered into computer databases, such as the LCCN and product code numbers (see Chapter 7); others appear only in the note area.

First level of description: all notes are optional.

Area 8: Standard Numbers and Terms of Availability

The eighth and final area of description is where ISBNs are entered along with information about bindings and paper, purchase or rental prices, etc. Because ISBNs can be searched as access points in computerized databases, it is important to enter them into catalog records. Some CIP records include qualifications enclosed in parentheses, such as the following: (hard cover or hc. or bound), (pbk.), and (alk. paper). If two ISBNs are given in the bibliographic record, qualifications are mandatory. Qualifications are optional when the bibliographic record has only one ISBN.

Terms of availability, such as price information, are optional, and many libraries choose not to include price because prices change over time. Should the policy of a library be to record prices in catalog records despite the limits on their accuracy, the price given should be the publisher's recommended list price, not the price actually paid for the item, which is likely to have been discounted by the seller.

ISBD punctuation for area 8:
- If the item has two or more ISBNs, these are separated by a period-space-dash-space. However, most CIPs list each ISBN in a separate paragraph, as also happens in a MARC record (see Chapter 7).

- Qualifications are enclosed in parentheses.

- Terms of availability are preceded by a space-colon-space.

Example: ISBN 978-1-932326-29-1 (alk. paper) : $24.95

First level of description: this information is required in both first and second level description.

The Concise AACR2

Michael Gorman, the editor of AACR2 for many years, has written *The Concise AACR2* (revised to the 2004 update) for cataloging department staff doing copy cataloging and small general libraries that need to have standard cataloging but don't need all the details of the full text. It explains in simplified terms the more generally applicable AACR2 rules for cataloging library materials. Beginning catalogers and library technicians might use this as a cataloging tool before consulting the much larger and more complex AACR2-2005.

The Future of Descriptive Cataloging

Since the publication of AACR2-2002, members of the Joint Steering Committee for Revision of AACR, subsequently renamed the Joint Steering Committee for Development of RDA (JSC), have been working on developing an entirely new descriptive cataloging code, titled *RDA: Resource Description and Access*. They seek to base RDA on a solid theoretical foundation rather than merely revising AACR2's existing rules and/or adding new rules to make it possible for catalogers to deal with new cataloging issues.

At this writing, RDA's publication is predicted in 2009 and its implementation by national libraries and large bibliographic networks in 2010. JSC claims that RDA's rules will be simpler, have fewer exceptions, and be written in such a way that catalogers can judge for themselves how to handle variations from the norm without causing problems in local catalogs or bibliographic databases extending beyond the local library. The aim of this rewriting of the cataloging code is to speed the cataloging process and make it possible for catalogers to respond to new problems without having to wait for years to obtain instructions from national libraries and library association committees on how to resolve these problems. Some of the principal changes expected: the arrangement of the rules by element rather than format; changes in terminology, for example, an edition statement will be called "an expression of a related manifestation"; fewer abbreviations will be allowed, for example, the abbreviation "col." will be written as either "color" or "colour" depending on the practice of the cataloging agency; ISBD punctuation will be optional; altering the way information about physical formats is expressed in catalog records; more optional rules; and other significant changes that will be noted in later chapters of this book.

It remains to be seen how much of a difference the new rules will make in the contents of records in library catalogs. Experts do not anticipate radical changes since one of RDA's stated aims is minimizing the need to alter preexisting records. Some experts have predicted that catalogers will continue to consult AACR2-2005.

Cataloging Tools Mentioned in Chapter 3

Anglo-American Cataloguing Rules, 2nd ed., 2002 revision, prepared under the direction of the Joint Steering Committee for Revision of AACR (Ottawa: Canadian Library Association; London: Chartered Institute of Library and Information Professionals; Chicago: American Library Association, 2002), plus updates issued in 2003, 2004, and 2005.

Cataloger's Desktop, Washington, DC: Library of Congress, Cataloging Distribution Service (http://www.desktop.loc.gov/).

Gorman, Michael. *The Concise AACR2: Based on AACR2 2002 Revision, 2004 Update*. 4th ed. (Chicago: American Library Association; Ottawa: Canadian Library Association; London: Chartered Institute of Library and Information Professionals, 2004).

Exercises

All the exercises below are for books that have one author as the main access point. Access points will be discussed in the next chapter. Also, do not add the tracings (subject headings and added access points); these will be discussed in future chapters. Answers to these exercises can be found in the Appendix.

Exercise 3A: Do first level and second level bibliographic records by completing the CIP information in Figure 2.1 on page 6 using the traditional bibliographic style. Note that the meaning of each line has been described on page 11.

This book is 19 cm. in height, has illustrations, and has 148 pages of text and xii preliminary pages.

Exercise 3B: Do first level and second level bibliographic records by completing the CIP information in Figure 2.2 on page 7 using the traditional bibliographic style. Note that the meaning of each line has been described on page 11.

This book is 24 cm. in height; has illustrations, some of which are colored; and has 276 pages of text and ix preliminary pages. It also has 32 pages of plates, which do not have page numbers.

Exercise 3C: Do first level and second level bibliographic records using the traditional bibliographic style by completing the CIP information for the following book by Stephen O'Shea, correcting the incorrect information in the CIP. The bibliographic references start on a page that is not numbered, but is actually page 385, and end on page 394.

This book is 24 cm. in height, has illustrations that include portraits and maps, and has 411 pages of text and xii preliminary pages.

(title page)

(information on verso)

SEA *of* FAITH

*Islam and Christianity
in the Medieval Mediterranean World*

STEPHEN O'SHEA

Walker & Company
New York

Copyright © 2006 by Stephen O'Shea

All rights reserved. No part of this book may be reproduced or transmitted in any form or by any means, electronic or mechanical, including photocopying, recording, or by any information storage and retrieval system, without permission in writing from the Publisher.

First published in the United States of America in 2006 by
Walker Publishing Company, Inc.
Distributed to the trade by Holtzbrinck Publishers

For information about permission to reproduce selections from this book, write to Permissions, Walker & Company, 104 Fifth Avenue, New York, New York 10011.

Maps by Tom Cross

Library of Congress Cataloging-in-Publication Data

O'Shea, Stephen.
Sea of faith : the shared story of Christianity and Islam in the medieval Mediterranean world / Stephen O'Shea.
p.   cm.
Includes bibliographical references (p.   ) and index.
ISBN-13: 978-0-8027-1498-5 (hardcover)
ISBN-10: 0-8027-1498-6 (hardcover)
1. Mediterranean Region—History, Military.   2. Islamic Empire—History, Military.   3. Europe—History, Military.   4. Battles—Mediterranean Region—History.   5. East and West.   I. Title.
DE84.O84   2006
909'.09822—dc22
2005033290

Visit Walker & Company's Web site at www.walkerbooks.com

Typeset by Westchester Book Group
Printed in the United States of America
by Quebecor World Fairfield

2 4 6 8 10 9 7 5 3 1

ISBN 0-8027-1498-6
ISBN-13 978-0-8027-1498-5

Exercise 3D: Do the descriptive cataloging for first level and second level bibliographic records using the traditional bibliographic style for the following book by Lynne Truss. It has no CIP. If you work in Canada, the publication, distribution area should reflect this fact.

This book is 20 cm. in height, has no illustrations, and has 209 pages of text and xxvii preliminary pages.

(title page)

Eats, Shoots & Leaves

The Zero Tolerance Approach to Punctuation

LYNNE TRUSS

GOTHAM BOOKS

(information on verso)

GOTHAM BOOKS
Published by Penguin Group (USA) Inc.
375 Hudson Street, New York, New York 10014, U.S.A.
Penguin Books Ltd, Registered Offices: 80 Strand, London WC2R 0RL, England
Penguin Books Australia Ltd, 250 Camberwell Road,
Camberwell, Victoria 3124, Australia
Penguin Books Canada Ltd, 10 Alcorn Avenue,
Toronto, Ontario, Canada M4V 3B2
Penguin Books (NZ) Ltd, Cnr Rosedale and Airborne Roads,
Albany, Auckland 1310, New Zealand

Published by Gotham Books, a division of Penguin Group (USA) Inc.

Originally published in Great Britain in 2003 by Profile Books, Ltd.
First American printing, April 2004

13 15 17 19 20 18 16

Copyright © 2003 by Lynne Truss
Foreword copyright © 2004 by Frank McCourt
All rights reserved

Gotham Books and the skyscraper logo are trademarks of Penguin Group (USA) Inc.

LIBRARY OF CONGRESS CATALOGING-IN-PUBLICATION DATA
has been applied for.

ISBN: 1-592-40087-6

Printed in the United States of America

Additional Information

4

Access Points

The choice of access points and their correct formulation is one of the most important parts of the cataloging process. Unlike Part I, all of AACR2-2005's Part II is used in cataloging books. Part II contains rules that instruct catalogers how to choose headings as access points to add to the bibliographic descriptions they have created and also how to put these headings into proper form. These include headings for persons, headings for corporate bodies, headings for geographic names, uniform titles, and references from variant forms of names.

Experts have predicted that the forthcoming *RDA: Resource Development and Access* will be generally compatible with AACR-2005 and that many of RDA's guidelines for choice and form of access points will not be different in essence from AACR-2005, but will be grouped and presented differently and include more information.

Two types of headings are derived from descriptive information: names and titles. Names are associated with the people and groups responsible for creating the intellectual or artistic content of materials being described. These people and groups include the primary "authors" and the other parties responsible for content, such as editors, illustrators, translators, and photographers. The names may be personal names or the names of groups of people acting together, known as "corporate bodies," such as the American Library Association. Some corporate body names involve geographic locations, for example, governments such as the province of "Ontario" or the federal government "United States."

Titles, which are, in fact, the "names" given to the content of works, include the titles of the materials being cataloged or series titles (larger material groups to which the books being cataloged belong).

"Main entry" and "added entry" are the terms used in AACR2-2005. In RDA, these terms will likely be changed to "primary access point" and "additional access point" and the distinction between "primary" and "additional" will be greatly reduced, although RDA will still have rules for creating primary access points if they are desired and needed to gather materials into bibliographies, etc. Computerized catalogs index all access points alike and respond to search inquiries the same way whether a search term is a main or added entry heading. In other words, access points are made for all names and titles that people might use in trying to find the work in the catalog. However, the designation of a main entry/primary access point is of importance for many libraries because the formulation of the book's call number that indicates the book's position on library shelves is linked to it. Call numbers are discussed in Chapter 6.

Choosing the Main Entry/Primary Access Point

The Anglo-American cataloging tradition is based on the assumption that the name of a work's creator is the work's most important identifying feature. Only one person, one corporate body, or one title can be chosen as the main entry. There are no "joint" main entries, even when two people or two corporate bodies share equal responsibility.

Most books are published by commercial firms. These firms are not normally responsible for the intellectual content of the works and, therefore, are not usually considered as possible access points. When a work "emanates" from a corporate body, it must first be determined if the work qualifies for a corporate body main entry. If it does, the corporate body is chosen as its main entry; if it does not, the decision goes back to the fundamental principle of attributing main entry to its creator. Thus, the choice of main entry begins by eliminating the possibility of corporate body main entry, even before seeking one or more creators of the material. The following decision tree illustrates the process:

1. Does the material emanate from a corporate body? There are four types of printed documents that are entered under a corporate body:
   a) an internal document of the corporate body, such as a library's catalog or an association's membership directory;
   b) an administrative document of the corporate body, such as an annual report;
   c) a document representing the collective thought of the body, such as minutes of a meeting or a report of a committee;
   d) a document representing the collective effort of a voyage, expedition, or conference.
   Yes: Enter the document under corporate body. (See Figure 4.5.)
   No: Go to step 3.

2. Are there two or three corporate bodies responsible for the work?
   Yes: Choose the first named body as the main entry.
   No: If there are more than three corporate bodies and no primary author, choose the title as the main entry.

3. Is one person primarily responsible for the work?
   Yes: Choose the person as the main entry. (See figures in Chapter 3.)
   No: Go to step 4.

4. Do two or three persons share the same primary responsibility?
   Yes: Choose the first named person as the main entry. (See Figure 4.1.)
   No: Choose the title as the main entry if more than three people share principal responsibility. (See Figure 4.2.)

5. Is this a work that has parts by different authors and is edited or compiled by one or more people?
   Yes: Choose the title as the main entry. (See Figure 4.3.)

6. Is the person or persons responsible for the item unknown?
   Yes: Choose the title as the main entry. (See Figure 4.4.)

Choosing Added Entries

When two or three people or bodies share principal responsibility for a work, make added entries/access points for the names not chosen as the main entry/access point. (See Figure 4.1.)

FIGURE 4.1

This example is an illustration of:
- joint responsibility
- bibliographic form of author's name taken from Library of Congress CIP
- other title information statement (in 2nd level cataloging)
- edition statement (in 2nd level cataloging)
- publishing date not listed; copyright date given
- detailed pagination
- descriptive illustration statement (in 2nd level cataloging)
- index note
- personal name added entry
- title added entry
- Library of Congress CIP

1st level cataloging

Spielman, A. (Andrew).
  Mosquito / by Andrew Spielman and Michael D'Antonio. -- Hyperion, c2001.
    xix, 247 p., [8] p. of plates

    ISBN 0-7868-6781-7.

  I. D'Antonio, Michael. II. Title.

2nd level cataloging

Spielman, A. (Andrew).
  Mosquito : a natural history of our most persistent and deadly foe / by Andrew Spielman and Michael D'Antonio. -- 1st ed. -- New York : Hyperion, c2001.
    xix, 247 p., [8] p. of plates : ill. (some col.), maps. ; 22 cm.

    Includes index.
    ISBN 0-7868-6781-7.

  I. D'Antonio, Michael. II. Title.

Fig. 4.1—Continues

However, if more than three people share equal responsibility and the title is chosen as the main entry, only the first person named is given in the statement of responsibility, followed by three dots (called marks of omission) and the phrase "et al." in square brackets. An added entry is made solely for the first named person. This instruction, called the Rule of Three, assumes that if searchers remember any of the names, they are most likely to remember the first. (See Figure 4.2.) It is expected that the Rule of Three will not be included in RDA and that all names can be listed and traced if desired.

FIGURE 4.1   *(continued)*

(title page)

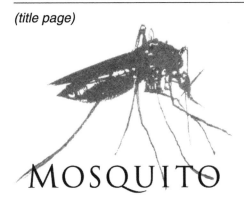

MOSQUITO

A NATURAL HISTORY OF OUR
MOST PERSISTENT AND DEADLY FOE

ANDREW SPIELMAN, Sc.D.,
AND MICHAEL D'ANTONIO

(information on verso)

Library of Congress Cataloging-in-Publication Data

Spielman, A. (Andrew)
    Mosquito : a natural history of our most persistent and deadly foe / by Andrew
Spielman and Michael D'Antonio.—1st ed.
        p.   cm.
    ISBN 0-7868-6781-7
        1. Mosquitoes.   2. Mosquitoes as carriers of disease.   I. D'Antonio, Michael.
    II. Title.
    QL536.S65 2001
    595.77'2—dc21   2001016815

Book design by Casey Hampton

FIRST EDITION

10 9 8 7 6 5 4 3 2 1

The content of a work that is edited or compiled is not considered to be the work of the editor(s) or compiler(s). Therefore, the main entry is under title and added entries are made for the compilers or editors (see Figure 4.3).

Other people or corporate bodies named in the statement of responsibility may also be given added entries depending on the likelihood that catalog users will search for their names. Translators and illustrators are frequently traced, but writers of introductions are not. However, in Figure 4.8 on page 53, Italo Calvino, the writer of the introduction, might be given an added entry in academic libraries because he is a prominent literary figure and catalog users might seek his minor writings.

Other added entries include the title proper (for books entered under persons or corporate authors) and title variations found outside the primary sources (such as cover titles and spine titles), series titles, and analytic titles. When a corporate body is named only in the publisher/distributor statement but has a close association with the intellectual contents of a work, an added entry is made for the corporate body (see Figure 4.4).

Establishing Proper Forms for Headings/Access Points

The process of establishing a proper form (called the "bibliographic form of name") for each person and corporate name heading in the catalog is known as "authority control." The purpose of authority control is to bring together under an authorized heading all the works by an individual or a corporate body. You will note in the CIP for Figure 4.1 that the name of the author given in the main entry heading differs from the manner in which his name is stated on the title page. This is because, at some time in the past, his

FIGURE 4.2

This example is an illustration of:
- item with more than three authors entered under title
- other title information (in 2nd level cataloging)
- marks of omission
- edition statement in both levels of cataloging to distinguish it from the U.S. edition
- detailed pagination statement
- index note (in 2nd level cataloging)
- ISBN qualified
- added entry for first author
- Library and Archives Canada CIP
- two levels of cataloging

1st level cataloging

```
The book of lists / by David Wallechinsky ... [et al.]. -- 1st
   Canadian ed. -- Knopf, 2005.
   x, 518 p.

   ISBN 0-676-97720-0 (pbk).

   I. Wallechinsky, David.
```

2nd level cataloging

```
The book of lists : the original compendium of curious
   information / by David Wallechinsky ... [et al.]. -- 1st
   Canadian ed. -- Toronto : Knopf, 2005.
   x, 518 p. : ill. ; 23 cm.

   Includes index.
   ISBN 0-676-97720-0 (pbk).

   I. Wallechinsky, David.
```

Fig. 4.2—Continues

name was "established" by the Library of Congress in this form and that form continues to be used in order to have all his works stand together in the catalog. There are other examples in this book in which the name of an author on the title page differs from the bibliographic form of that name in the CIP record.

Sometimes, a book contains two CIPs because the publisher has submitted cataloging data to two authoritative libraries. Such dual CIPs are found in Figure 2.3 on page 8. The Library of Congress and the National Library of Canada, (that is, the Library and Archives of Canada) have established different forms of the author's name. In order to decide which form to use, a cataloger consults an authority file, generally a computerized database. If the library has a local authority file, this should be consulted first. In some libraries, it is a

FIGURE 4.2 *(continued)*

| *(title page)* | *(information on verso)* |

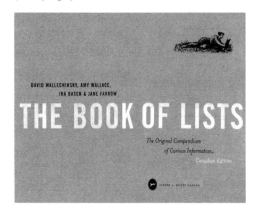

PUBLISHED BY ALFRED A. KNOPF CANADA

Original edition copyright © 1977, 1980, 1983, 2004 David Wallechinsky and Amy Wallace
Canadian edition copyright © 2005 Ira Basen and Jane Farrow
Published by agreement with Canongate Books Ltd., Edinburgh, Scotland

www.randomhouse.ca

Photo Credits
Chapter 1–Copyright © *The People's Almanac* Photographic Archives; Chapter 2–Film still from *McKenna of the Mounted* ; Chapter 3–Library and Archives Canada/ Credit: Duncan Cameron (PA–180804); Chapter 4–Paul V. Galvin Library collection; Chapter 5–Library and Archives Canada/ Credit: Claude-Charles Bacqueville de La Potherie (CFC305 B326); Chapter 6–City of Vancouver Archives, CVA 1184–2559; Chapter 7–Copyright © Frank Micoletta/Getty Image; Chapter 8–Steve Patterson/Glaucomys.org; Chapter 9–Jeff Goode/*Toronto Star*; Chapter 10–Copyright © M. Ponomareff/PonoPresse; Chapter 11–Copyright © Brian Willer - Toronto; Chapter 12–J.H. Webster/Hudson's Bay Co. Archives/Archives of Manitoba (HBCA 1987/363-E-152/4); Chapter 13–Library and Archives Canada/Montreal Star collection (PA-209767); Chapter 14–Niagara Falls (Ont.) Public Library - Digital Collections - George Bailey; Chapter 15–Saskatchewan Archives Board (S-B4121)

Pages 506 to 507 constitute a continuation of the copyright page. Also included is a key to contributors.

LIBRARY AND ARCHIVES CANADA CATALOGUING IN PUBLICATION

The book of lists / David Wallechinsky ... [et al.]. – Canadian ed.

Includes index.
ISBN 0-676-97720-0

1. Handbooks, vade-mecums, etc. 2. Curiosities and wonders.
3. Curiosities and wonders–Canada. I. Wallechinsky, David, 1948– .

AG106.B66 2005   031.02   C2005-901023-1

Text design: CS Richardson

First Canadian Edition

Printed and bound in the United States of America

10 9 8 7 6 5 4 3 2 1

network authority file shared by network partners. The largest and most widely used authority file in North America is the Library and Archives of Canada-Library of Congress-Program for Cooperative Cataloging Name Authority File (NAF), available from LAC, LC, OCLC, and other sources. One might assume that "Name Authority File" means that the file is limited to names; however, authorized forms of uniform titles (discussed later in this chapter) and series titles are included in it as well as personal and corporate body names. Although LC ceased to support series in the authority file in 2006, other U.S. contributors continue to do so, and LAC still maintains its series authorities. LC authorities can be accessed at http://authorities.loc.gov. For details about accessing LAC authorities, see http://collectionscanada.gc.ca/libraries/index-e.html.

FIGURE 4.3

This example is an illustration of:
- edited work entered under title
- publishing date not listed; copyright date given
- detailed pagination
- series statement (in 2nd level cataloging)
- index note (in 2nd level cataloging)
- ISBN qualified
- added entries for editors
- series added entry
- Library of Congress CIP

1st level cataloging

New media, 1740-1915 / edited by Lisa Gitelman and Geoffrey B.
  Pingree. -- MIT Press, c2003.
  xxxiii, 271 p.

  ISBN 0-262-07245-9 (hc. : alk. paper).

  I. Gitelman, Lisa.   II. Pingree, Geoffrey B.

2nd level cataloging

New media, 1740-1915 / edited by Lisa Gitelman and Geoffrey B.
  Pingree. -- Cambridge, Mass. : Pingree, c2003.
  xxxiii, 271 p. ; 23 cm. -- (Media in transition)

  Includes index.
  ISBN 0-262-07245-9 (hc. : alk. paper).

  I. Gitelman, Lisa.   II. Pingree, Geoffrey B.   III. Series.

Fig. 4.3—Continues

Form of Personal Names

AACR2-2005 authorizes the name form most likely to be known to users of the catalog, that is, the form that appears most frequently in the person's works or by which he or she is most commonly known. Applying this test to the creators of *Tom Sawyer* and *Alice's Adventures in Wonderland*, catalogers select Mark Twain and Lewis Carroll, respectively, not Samuel Langhorne Clemens or Charles Lutwidge Dodgson, as the authorized headings. An example of exceptions made to the rules that authorize multiple headings for a single individual is a person who uses different names on works in different genres (Charles Dodgson published nonfiction works under his real name, but adopted a pseudonym, Lewis Carroll, for his books of fiction).

AACR2-2005 has rules for establishing name forms in many languages in addition to English. They are formulated as they would be listed in authoritative alphabetical listings

FIGURE 4.3 *(continued)*

(title page)

New Media, 1740–1915

Edited by Lisa Gitelman and Geoffrey B. Pingree

The MIT Press
Cambridge, Massachusetts
London, England

(information on verso)

This book was set in Perpetua by Graphic Composition, Inc.

Printed and bound in the United States of America.

Library of Congress Cataloging-in-Publication Data
New media, 1740–1915 / edited by Lisa Gitelman and Geoffrey B. Pingree.
    p. cm. — (Media in transition)
    Includes bibliographical references and index.
    ISBN 0-262-07245-9 (hc. : alk. paper)
    1. Mass media—History. I. Gitelman, Lisa. II. Pingree, Geoffrey B. III. Series.

P90 .N5 2003
302.23'09—dc21
                                                                    2002029542

10 9 8 7 6 5 4 3 2

(information on series)

Media in Transition
David Thorburn, series editor
Edward Barrett, Henry Jenkins, associate editors

New Media, 1740–1915, edited by Lisa Gitelman and Geoffrey B. Pingree, 2003

Democracy and New Media, edited by Henry Jenkins and David Thorburn, 2003

Rethinking Media Change: The Aesthetics of Transition, edited by David Thorburn and Henry Jenkins, 2003

(information on bar code)

in their home countries. For English-language names, the rule of thumb is to enter a name that contains a surname under the surname, followed by a comma and the forename(s) in direct order (for example, Jones, Constance). Surnames may consist of a single element (John Doe), two elements connected by a hyphen (Barbara Smith-Brown), or multiple elements without hyphens (Catherine St. Armand, Joseph de Villiers). When English-language names are hyphenated, the surname is filed under the first element, for example, Barbara Smith-Brown is filed in the S's as "Smith-Brown, Barbara," *not* in the B's as "Brown, Barbara Smith." English-language names with compound surnames are usually entered under the first element, for example, "St. Armand, Catherine" and "De Villiers, Joseph."

LC and LAC name authority files give the fullest form of personal names because their collections are so large that they are likely to contain similar names. Smaller libraries can use these fuller forms to distinguish the works of authors when an author's name given on a title page is the same as that of another author listed in the catalog. For example, the bibliographic name of two authors called J. E. Doe might be Doe, J. E. (John Edward) and Doe, J. E. (Jane Eleanor). Birth and death dates can also be used to distinguish authors with

FIGURE 4.4

This example is an illustration of:
- title main entry
- other title information(in 2nd level cataloging)
- publishing date not listed; copyright date given
- detailed pagination
- bibliography and index note (in 2nd level cataloging)
- ISBN qualified
- added entry for corporate body (form of name taken from the established form in the Library of Congress CIP)

1st level cataloging

```
The film preservation guide. -- National Film Preservation
   Foundation, c2004.
   xi, 121 p.

   ISBN 0-9747099-0-5 (alk. paper).

   I. National Film Preservation Foundation (U.S.).
```

2nd level cataloging

```
The film preservation guide : the basics for archives, libraries,
   and museums. -- San Francisco : National Film Preservation
   Foundation, c2004.
   xi, 121 p. : ill. ; 24 cm.

   Includes bibliographical references and index.
   ISBN 0-9747099-0-5 (alk. paper).

   I. National Film Preservation Foundation (U.S.).
```

Fig. 4.4—Continues

similar names. These dates have not been added to the bibliographic form of names in the catalog records in this book even when given in CIP data to demonstrate that such dates are required only if it is part of a library's policy.

Special rules cover names that include titles of nobility, names that do not include surnames but contain patronymics, names of kings and queens, and other special cases.

Form of Corporate Body Names

The same principle that guides the formulation of personal names—the most frequently encountered form—guides the formulation of corporate body names as well as their verification in the same authority lists. Corporate names are more likely than personal names to change. For example, over the years, the University of Toronto has changed the

FIGURE 4.4 *(continued)*

(title page)

THE FILM PRESERVATION GUIDE
THE BASICS FOR ARCHIVES, LIBRARIES, AND MUSEUMS

National Film Preservation Foundation
San Francisco, California

(information on verso)

National Film Preservation Foundation
870 Market Street, Suite 1113
San Francisco, CA 94102

© 2004 by the National Film Preservation Foundation

Library of Congress Cataloging-in-Publication Data
    The film preservation guide : the basics for archives, libraries, and museums.
        p. cm.
    Includes bibliographical references and index.
    ISBN 0-9747099-0-5 (alk. paper)
    1. Motion picture film—Preservation. I. National Film Preservation Foundation (U.S.)
TR886.3F58   2003
778.5'8—dc22   2003024032
                                                                                  CIP

This publication was made possible through a grant from The Andrew W. Mellon Foundation. It
may be downloaded as a PDF file from the National Film Preservation Foundation Web site:
www.filmpreservation.org.

Credits
Except as noted below, all photographs were provided by Barbara Galasso and the L. Jeffrey Selznick
School of Film Preservation at George Eastman House. The following contributed illustrations and
text material: American Museum of Natural History (94), Anonymous (67), California Pacific Medical
Center (57), Chace Productions Inc. (12 center and right), Duke University (48 top), Estate of Edith
Lutyens Bel Geddes and the Harry Ransom Humanities Research Center at the University of Texas at
Austin (84), Florida Moving Image Archive (91), Image Permanence Institute at the Rochester Institute
of Technology (10 top), Library of Congress (48 bottom, 51, 63, 87), Minnesota Historical Society
(92), National Center for Jewish Film (90), Nebraska State Historical Society (69, 73, 74), Northeast
Historic Film (back cover, 62 bottom, 76, 85), Oklahoma Historical Society (5), Pacific Film Archive at
the University of California at Berkeley (back cover), Sabucat Productions (93), UCLA Film and Tele-
vision Archive (86), University of Alaska Fairbanks (40), University of South Carolina Newsfilm Library
(89), Visual Communications (58).

Typesetting by David Wells
Copyediting by Sylvia Tan
Printed in the USA by Great Impressions

name Library School to Faculty of Library Science, to Faculty of Information Studies, to its present Faculty of Information.

While beginning catalogers are unlikely to establish complicated corporate names, it is important to understand how they are determined. The principal complication in determining the proper form of corporate body names is that some bodies are part of larger entities. This raises the problem of whether to enter such bodies under their own names or under the names of the parent bodies (called a "subordinate" entry). The Association for Library Collections & Technical Services (ALCTS), the division of the American Library Association responsible for cataloging and classification, provides a good example of how the rules guide the decisions. Even though it is a division of a larger body, ALCTS' name does not imply that subordination, so it is entered under its own name. Before 1990, however, ALCTS' name was Resources and Technical Services Division (RTSD). Because this former name implied subordination, RTSD was entered indirectly under the name of the larger association: *American Library Association. Resources and Technical Services Division.*

AACR2-2005 instructs catalogers to formulate corporate body names subordinately, under the name of a larger or parent body, for six types of names:

1. The name contains a term that implies it is part of another, such as "Division," "Department," etc. The heading for RTSD, above, is an example.

2. The name contains a word normally associated with administrative subordination, such as "Committee" or "Commission," for example: *Ex Libris Association. Nominating Committee.*

3. The name is general in nature, indicating only a geographic, chronological, numbered, or lettered subdivision, such as "Class of 2008," for example: *Clearwater College. Class of 2008.* (Note: this is a fictitious example.)

4. The name does not convey the idea of a corporate body, such as "Public Relations," for example: *BankAmerica International. Public Relations.* (Note: this is a fictitious example.)

5. The name is a university faculty, school, college, etc., for example: *University of Toronto. Faculty of Information.*

6. The name includes the entire name of the parent body, such as "Harvard University Libraries," for example: *Harvard University. Libraries.*

Still more complicated are bodies that include many layers of hierarchy, such as the Committee on Cataloging: Description and Access (CC:DA), the committee concerned with descriptive cataloging rules. It is a committee of a section of a division of an association, as follows:

American Library Association (parent body)
    Association for Library Collections & Technical Services (division)
        Cataloging and Classification Section (section of the division)
            Committee on Cataloging: Description and Access (committee of the section)

In the case of multiple layers, the body is entered under the name of the lowest unit of hierarchy that can stand alone, provided it is a unique identification. For CC:DA, the heading form would be under ALCTS, which is the lowest body that can stand alone, and the intervening section, Cataloging and Classification Section, would not be included because there is no other committee by the same name in any other section of ALCTS: *Association for Library Collections & Technical Services. Committee on Cataloging: Description and Access.* (Note that an ampersand is used in the name of the association, but not in the name of the section or the committee because this is the way these entities are known.)

If an initial article accompanies the name of a corporate body on a document, it is omitted from a heading unless the article is an important filing element, such as "Los Angeles." Special rules in AACR2-2005 cover heading forms for governments, government bodies, government officials, religions, religious bodies and religious officials, conferences and similar events, etc.

A beginning cataloger would not be expected to formulate the name of the corporate body in Figure 4.5. However, if the library's catalog lists another book of this corporate body's conference proceedings from other years, the cataloger can use the bibliographic form of that name and substitute the conference number, year, and place where it was held to fashion a new heading suitable to the book in hand.

FIGURE 4.5

This example is an illustration of:
- named conference
- entry under corporate body
- two other title information statements (in 2nd level description)
- joint editors
- publication date not listed, copyright date given
- edition and history as a quoted note
- bibliography and index note (in 2nd level description)
- ISBN qualified
- added entries for editors
- Library of Congress CIP

1st level cataloging

North American Serials Interest Group. Conference (17th : 2002 :
    College of William and Mary)
  Transforming serials / Susan L. Scheiberg, Shelley Neville, editors.
-- Haworth, c2003.
  365 p.

  "Co-published simultaneously as The serials librarian, v. 44, nos.
1/2 and 3/4 (2003)."
  ISBN 0-7890-2282-6 (pbk. : alk paper).

  I. Scheiberg, Susan. II. Neville, Shelley. III. Serials librarian.
IV. Title.

2nd level cataloging

North American Serials Interest Group. Conference (17th : 2002 :
    College of William and Mary)
  Transforming serials : the revolution continues : proceedings of the
North American Serials Interest Group, Inc. 17th Annual Conference,
June 20-23, 2002, the College of William and Mary, Williamsburg,
Virginia / Susan L. Scheiberg, Shelley Neville, editors. -- New York :
Haworth, c2003.
  365 p. ; 21 cm.

  "Co-published simultaneously as The serials librarian, v. 44, nos.
1/2 and 3/4 (2003)".
  Includes bibliographical references and index.
  ISBN 0-7890-2282-6 (pbk. : alk paper).

  I. Scheiberg, Susan. II. Neville, Shelley. III. Serials librarian.
IV. Title.

Fig. 4.5—Continues

FIGURE 4.5 *(continued)*

(title page)

**TRANSFORMING SERIALS:
THE REVOLUTION CONTINUES**

**Proceedings of the
NORTH AMERICAN SERIALS
INTEREST GROUP, Inc.**

**17th Annual Conference
June 20-23, 2002
The College of William and Mary
Williamsburg, Virginia**

Susan L. Scheiberg
Shelley Neville
Editors

The Haworth Information Press
An Imprint of
The Haworth Press, Inc.
New York • London • Oxford

(information on verso)

Transforming Serials: The Revolution Continues has been co-published simultaneously as *The Serials Librarian*, Volume 44, Numbers 1/2 and 3/4 2003.

The development, preparation, and publication of this work has been undertaken with great care. However, the publisher, employees, editors, and agents of The Haworth Press and all imprints of The Haworth Press, Inc., including The Haworth Medical Press® and Pharmaceutical Products Press®, are not responsible for any errors contained herein or for consequences that may ensue from use of materials or information contained in this work. Opinions expressed by the author(s) are not necessarily those of The Haworth Press, Inc.

Cover design by Thomas J. Mayshock Jr.

Library of Congress Cataloging-in-Publication Data

North American Serials Interest Group. Conference (17th : 2002 : College of William and Mary)
      Transforming serials : the revolution continues : proceedings of the North American Serials Interest Group, Inc. 17th Annual Conference, June 20-23, 2002, the College of William and Mary, Williamsburg, Virginia / Susan L. Scheiberg, Shelley Neville, editors.
         p. cm.
"Co-published simultaneously as The serials librarian, v. 44, nos. 1/2 and 3/4 2003."
Includes bibliographical references and index.
      ISBN 0-7890-2281-8 (alk. paper) – ISBN 0-7890-2282-6 (pbk : alk. paper)
1. Serials librarianship–Congresses. 2. Libraries–Special collections–Electronic journals–Congresses. 3. Electronic journals–Congresses. I. Scheiberg, Susan L. II. Neville, Shelley. III. Serials librarian. IV. Title.
      Z692.S5N67 2002
      025.17′32–dc21   2003005542

FIGURE 4.6

This example is an illustration of:
- title note
- edition and history note(in 2nd level cataloging)
- two title added entries
- National Library of Canada (i.e., Library and Archives of Canada) CIP

1st level cataloging

```
Visser, Margaret.
  Much depends on dinner. -- Harper Perennial, 1992.
  351 p.

  Title on cover: Since Eve ate apples-much depends on dinner.
  ISBN 1-55263-347-0.

  I. Title.  II. Title: Since Eve ate apples-much depends on dinner.
```

2nd level cataloging

```
Visser, Margaret.
  Much depends on dinner / Margaret Visser. -- Toronto ; Harper
Perennial, 1992.
  351 p. ; 23 cm.

  Title on cover: Since Eve ate apples-much depends on dinner : the
extraordinary history and mythology, allure and obsessions, perils and
taboos, of an ordinary meal.
  First published by McClelland and Stewart, 1986.
  ISBN 1-55263-347-0.

  I. Title.  II. Title: Since Eve ate apples-much depends on dinner.
```

Note: Title on cover note in 2nd level cataloging also functions as a summary note.

Fig. 4.6—Continues

Forms of Geographic Names

Geographic names appear in catalogs as descriptive headings, generally as the first part of the name of a governmental body or official. The English form of the name of a place is chosen if there is one in general use; if there is doubt about the existence of an English form in general use, the form used by the people in that place (the vernacular form) is preferred.

Geographic names may have more than one standardized form because of official changes to the names of cities and towns as well as entire countries. A good example is Germany. In a library collection with government documents relating to twentieth-century

FIGURE 4.6 *(continued)*

(information on cover)

Fig. 4.6—Continues

Germany, the form of name for Germany might have eight different headings because of its division into occupied zones after World War II, its split into East and West Germany, and its eventual reunification. The catalog must represent the publications of each one under the heading appropriate to it.

The second problem, multiple locations that share the same name, is solved by adding elements to the basic name that create unique headings for each location. Two kinds of elements may be added, depending on the type of location. If it is a place name in a country, the name of the country is added, or, for localities in Australia, Canada, the United States, and several other countries, the name of a state, province, or part of the British Isles is added to it, for example, Bangor (Wales), Bangor (Northern Ireland), and Bangor (Maine). If the places are countries, then dates or other terms may be added to indicate the country at a particular point in time or under a particular government, such as Vichy France during World War II, known as France (Territory under German occupation, 1940–1944).

Forms of Titles

Titles Proper

Titles proper are entered the way they appear in the first area of description and, with a few exceptions, are traced. Computer indexing can be coded to ignore the initial articles

FIGURE 4.6 *(continued)*

(title page)

MUCH DEPENDS on DINNER

(information on verso)

First published by McClelland and Stewart: 1986
First HarperPerennial edition: 1992

Canadian Cataloguing in Publication Data

Visser, Margaret, 1940-
   Much depends on dinner

Includes bibliographical references and index.
ISBN 0-00-637759-9

1. Food habits — Social aspects. 2. Food — Social aspects. 3. Food — History. 4. Food — Folklore. I. Title.

GT2855.V57 1992   641   C92-093092-1

92 93 94 95 96 GP 5 4 3 2 1

Illustrations by Mary Firth

MARGARET VISSER

HarperPerennial
HarperCollins*PublishersLtd*

and file on the first significant word, so a title such as *The Library at Night* files as if it were *Library at Night*. The Library of Congress once followed a policy of not making title proper headings if they included words such as "Fundamentals of the . . . ," "A History of the . . . ," or "An Introduction to the . . . ," because they were difficult to search successfully in card files. Computerized searching, using both title keywords and entering whole titles, has made such titles readily accessible. Most catalogers now make title proper headings routinely.

One frequently encountered additional access point is making added entries containing spelled out versions of title words that appear on chief sources as digits, ampersands, or other symbols. If this is not done, searchers entering the title with spelled out words,

FIGURE 4.7

This example is an illustration of:
- bibliographic form of author's name taken from CIP record
- uniform title (in 2nd record)
- other title information
- statement of subsidiary responsibility
- detailed pagination statement
- descriptive illustration statement
- edition and history note (in 1st record)
- bibliography and index note
- two title added entries
- Library of Congress CIP
- two methods of cataloging a book published with different titles

2nd level cataloging without a uniform title

MacMillan, Margaret Olwen.
   Paris 1919 : six months that changed the world / Margaret MacMillan ; foreword by Richard Holbrooke. -- New York : Random House, 2003.
   xxxi, 570 p., [16] p. of plates : ill., maps, ports. ; 23 cm.

   Originally published: Peacemakers. London: J. Murray, 2001.
   Includes bibliographical references and index.
   ISBN 0—375-76052-0.

   I. Title. II. Title: Peacemakers.

2nd level cataloging with a uniform title

MacMillan, Margaret Olwen.
   [Peacemakers]
   Paris 1919 : six months that changed the world / Margaret MacMillan ; foreword by Richard Holbrooke. -- New York : Random House, 2003.
   xxxi, 570 p. [16] p. of plates : ill., maps, ports. ; 23 cm.

   Includes bibliographical references and index.
   ISBN 0—375-76052-0.

   I. Title. II. Title: Peacemakers.

Note: Publication, distribution statement in Canada would be:

New York : Random House, 2003.

Fig. 4.7—Continues

thinking that librarians do not use digits and symbols in the catalog, could fail to find the material even though it is part of the collection. For example, a title added entry would be made for the title on the title page, *The cat & its friends*, as well as an additional title added entry for *The cat and its friends*.

FIGURE 4.7 *(continued)*

(title page)

PARIS

SIX MONTHS THAT CHANGED THE WORLD

1919

Margaret MacMillan

FOREWORD BY
Richard Holbrooke

RANDOM HOUSE TRADE PAPERBACKS
NEW YORK

(information on verso)

2003 Random House Trade Paperback Edition

Copyright © 2001 by Margaret MacMillan
Foreword copyright © 2002 by Richard Holbrooke
Maps copyright © 2002 by Jeffrey L. Ward

This work was originally published in Great Britain, in slightly different
form, as *Peacemakers*, by John Murray (Publishers) Ltd. in 2001, and in hardcover as *Paris 1919*
by Random House, an imprint of The Random House Publishing Group, a division
of Random House, Inc., New York, in 2002.

The author and publisher would like to thank the following for permission to
reproduce illustrations: Plates 1 and 7, Princeton University Library; 2, 4, 5, 8, 9,
11, 12, 13, 16, 17, 20, 21, 22, 23, 24, 27 and 28, Hulton Getty; 3 and 29, The Trustees
of the Imperial War Museum, London; 10, 14, 18, 25 and 26, *The Illustrated
London News* Picture Library; 15, 19 and 30, Mary Evans Picture Library.

LIBRARY OF CONGRESS CATALOGING-IN-PUBLICATION DATA
MacMillan, Margaret Olwen.
[Peacemakers]
Paris 1919 : six months that changed the world / Margaret MacMillan.
p. cm.
Originally published: Peacemakers. London : J. Murray, 2001.
Includes bibliographical references and index.
ISBN 0-375-76052-0
1. Paris Peace Conference (1919–1920) 2. World War, 1914–1918—Peace.
3. Treaty of Versailles (1919) 4. Germany—History—1918–1933.
5. Wilson, Woodrow, 1856–1924. 6. Germany—Boundaries. I. Title.
D644 .M32 2002
940.3′141—dc21   2002023707

Random House website address: www.atrandom.com
Printed in the United States of America

468975

Book design by Casey Hampton

Another additional access point is made when the words of other title information, such as a subtitle, are displayed on the title page more prominently in larger and or darker print than the title proper. A catalog user could easily believe the larger and or darker type is the title proper. A variation of the title found elsewhere on the book could also be misleading. For example, the book jacket in Figure 4.6 appears to start with the title "Since Eve Ate Apples," and some catalog users may assume that this is the title of the book they seek.

Uniform Titles

In some CIP records, there is a line in square brackets between the main entry/access point and the title proper. This is called a uniform title. Uniform titles are optional and are generally constructed by libraries with large collections to bring together all versions of a work known by more than one title. For example, the uniform title in the CIP in Figure 4.7 brings together in the catalog all versions of this work published under different titles.

FIGURE 4.8

This example is an illustration of:
- fiction book
- uniform title (in 2nd record)
- two statements of subsidiary responsibility
- date of publication uncertain (the 13-digit ISBN started in 2007, book received 2008)
- detailed pagination
- edition and history note (in 1st record)
- ISBN qualified
- personal name added entries
- two title added entries
- optional use of designation in added entry (in 1st record)
- Library of Congress CIP corrected for order of subsidiary statements of responsibility
- two methods of cataloging a translated book

2nd level cataloging without a uniform title

Gadda, Carlo Emilio.
   That awful mess on the Via Merulana / by Carlo Emilio Gadda ;
translated from the Italian by William Weaver ; introduction by Italo
Calvino. -- New York : New York Review Books, [2007 or 2008].
   xxi, 388 p. ; 21 cm. -- (New York Review Books classics)

   Translation of: Quer pasticciaccio brutto de via Merilana.
   ISBN 978-1—59017-22-3 (alk. paper).

   I. Weaver, William, tr.   II. Calvino, Italo.   III. Title.   IV. Title:
Quer pasticciaccio brutto de via Merilana.

2nd level cataloging with a uniform title

Gadda, Carlo Emilio.
   [Quer pasticciaccio brutto de via Merilana. English.]
   That awful mess on the Via Merulana / by Carlo Emilio Gadda ;
translated from the Italian by William Weaver ; introduction by Italo
Calvino. -- New York : New York Review Books, [2007 or 2008].
   xxi, 388 p. ; 21 cm. -- (New York Review Books classics)

   ISBN 978-1—59017-22-3 (alk. paper)

   I. Weaver, William.   II. Calvino, Italo.   III. Title.   IV. Title:
Quer pasticciaccio brutto de via Merilana.

Fig. 4.8—Continues

   Figure 4.8 is a second example of the use of uniform tiles. Here the uniform title,
shown in the CIP, collocates versions of a foreign language work. Uniform titles are usually
not constructed by beginning catalogers.

FIGURE 4.8 *(continued)*

(title page)

THAT AWFUL MESS
ON THE VIA MERULANA   *(information on verso)*

THIS IS A NEW YORK REVIEW BOOK
PUBLISHED BY THE NEW YORK REVIEW OF BOOKS
1755 Broadway, New York, NY 10019
www.nyrb.com

CARLO EMILIO GADDA

Published in Italian as *Quer pasticciaccio brutto de via Merulana*

Translated from the Italian by

WILLIAM WEAVER

Library of Congress Cataloging-in-Publication Data
Gadda, Carlo Emilio, 1893–1973.
   [Quer pasticciaccio brutto de via Merulana. English]
   That awful mess on the Via Merulana / by Carlo Emilio Gadda ; introduction
by Italo Calvino ; translated by William Weaver.
       p. cm. — (New York Review Books classics)
   ISBN 978-1-59017-222-3 (alk. paper)
   I. Weaver, William, 1923– II. Title.
PQ4817.A33Q413 2007
853'.912—dc22

                                              2006036813

Introduction by

ITALO CALVINO

ISBN 978-1-59017-222-3

Printed in the United States of America on acid-free paper.
10 9 8 7 6 5 4 3 2 1

NEW YORK REVIEW BOOKS

New York

Analytic Titles

Analytic titles appearing in contents notes may or may not be given added entries/access points, often depending on a library's policy or whether these titles are likely to be searched individually by patrons (for example, three novellas presented together in one volume) or if there are a great many (for example, poems in an anthology). A library may decide to include only some of the analytic titles in the contents note. In this case, the contents note will begin with "Partial contents" as shown in Figure 4.9.

The added entries for analytic titles may be made as name-title headings, that is, headings that begin with the name of the creator (in authorized form) followed by the title proper of the work or as single titles. For example, the added entries for Figure 3.3 on page 19 could be:

I. Aristotle. Politics. II. Aristotle. Poetics. III. Jowett, Benjamin, tr.   IV. Twining, Thomas, tr.   V. Title. VI. Title: Poetics.

FIGURE 4.9

```
This example is an illustration of:
    • subsidiary responsibility
    • detailed pagination
    • series statement
    • partial contents note
    • bibliography note
    • added entry for editor
    • title added entries
    • Library of Congress CIP
    • 2nd level cataloging


Dickens, Charles.
  Christmas books / Charles Dickens ; edited with an introduction and
notes by Ruth Glancy. -- Oxford ; New York : Oxford University Press,
1998.
  xxv, 486 p. ; 20 cm. -- (Oxford world's classics)

  Partial contents: A Christmas carol -- The chimes -- The cricket on
the hearth -- The battle of life -- The haunted man.
  Includes bibliography.
  ISBN 0-19-283435-5.

  I. Glancy, Ruth.   II. Title.   III. Title: A Christmas carol.
IV. Title: The chimes.   V. Title: The cricket on the hearth.
VI. Title: The battle of life.   VII. Title: The haunted man.


N.B.   If catalogued in Canada, the publication distribution area would
read: Oxford ; Toronto : Oxford University Press, 1998.

The CIP has the uniform title [Novels. Selections].  This uniform title
might be used in large collections of Dickens works.  See pages 52-53
for a discussion of uniform titles.
```

Fig. 4.9—Continues

Series Titles

Series titles are not always given added entries, depending on local policy. Some libraries and media centers trace only scholarly series; some trace selected series decided on a case-by-case basis; some trace all series. Most libraries are selective. For example, the series in Figure 4.8 would not be traced because there are very many books in this series and they do not have any relation to each other than the fact that the publisher considers each of them a classic of some sort. However, the series in the second level description in Figure 4.3 on page 41 would be traced because the books in that series all relate to the same subject and people may be interested in reading the others.

FIGURE 4.9 *(continued)*

(information on verso)

OXFORD
UNIVERSITY PRESS

Great Clarendon Street, Oxford OX2 6DP

Oxford University Press is a department of the University of Oxford.
It furthers the University's objective of excellence in research, scholarship,
and education by publishing worldwide in

Oxford New York

Athens Auckland Bangkok Bogotá Buenos Aires Cape Town
Chennai Dar es Salaam Delhi Florence Hong Kong Istanbul Karachi
Kolkata Kuala Lumpur Madrid Melbourne Mexico City Mumbai Nairobi
Paris São Paulo Shanghai Singapore Taipei Tokyo Toronto Warsaw
with associated companies in Berlin Ibadan

Oxford is a registered trade mark of Oxford University Press
in the UK and in certain other countries

Published in the United States
by Oxford University Press Inc., New York

Introduction, Notes on the Text, Explanatory Notes, Further Reading
© Ruth Glancy 1988
Chronology © Kathleen Tillotson 1982

The moral rights of the author have been asserted

Database right Oxford University Press (maker)

First published as a World's Classics paperback 1988
Reissued as an Oxford World's Classics paperback 1998

All rights reserved. No part of this publication may be reproduced,
stored in a retrieval system, or transmitted, in any form or by any means,
without the prior permission in writing of Oxford University Press,
or as expressly permitted by law, or under terms agreed with the appropriate
reprographics rights organizations. Enquiries concerning reproduction
outside the scope of the above should be sent to the Rights Department,
Oxford University Press, at the address above

You must not circulate this book in any other binding or cover
and you must impose this same condition on any acquirer

British Library Cataloguing in Publication Data
Data available

Library of Congress Cataloging in Publication Data
Dickens, Charles, 1812–1870.
[Novels, Selections]
Christmas Books / Charles Dickens; edited with an introduction by
Ruth Glancy.
p.   cm.—(Oxford world's classics)
Bibliography: p.
Contents: Note on the text—A Chronology of Charles Dickens—A
Christmas carol—The chimes—The cricket on the hearth—The
battle of life—The haunted man.
1. Christmas stories. I. Glancy, Ruth F., 1948–   . II. Title.
PR4557.A1 1988 823'.8—dc   88–14170
ISBN 0–19–283435–5

3 5 7 9 10 8 6 4

Printed in Great Britain by
Cox & Wyman Ltd.
Reading, Berkshire

(title page)

OXFORD WORLD'S CLASSICS

═══

CHARLES DICKENS

Christmas Books

═══

Edited with an Introduction and Notes by
RUTH GLANCY

OXFORD
UNIVERSITY PRESS

CONTENTS

Series statements that are wanted as access points are usually traced exactly as they appear on the material being cataloged, following rules almost identical to those for recording titles proper.

However, series added entries might not be identical to the series titles given in the series statement. Beginning catalogers should search the library's name authority file to see if a series title heading has been established for the series. If a book was published in 2006 or later, do not search for a series authority record in the authority file maintained by the Library of Congress because LC discontinued its practice of establishing new series headings at that time. The Library and Archives of Canada has maintained its series authority.

If the heading is not found, the cataloger should next search the library's catalog for other titles in the series and follow the manner in which the library has dealt with the series. If other books in the series are not listed in the catalog, the beginning cataloger should give this bibliographic record to an experienced cataloger to finish.

Name Cross-References

A "see" reference leads a searcher from unauthorized names and name forms to the authorized name form. "See" or "See also" references are made for

- Different names for the same person, for example, Munro, Hector Hugh, *see* Saki, but Dodgson, Charles Lutwidge, *see also* Carroll, Lewis (who wrote under both names).

- Different forms of a name, for example, Weihs, Jean, *see* Weihs, Jean Riddle.

- Different entry elements, for example, Mare, Walter de la, *see* De la Mare, Walter.

These simple "see" references can easily be made by beginning catalogers. The more complicated cross-references—name-title references (headings that include a name plus a title), geographic name references, corporate body references, most "see also" references, differences in name forms caused by languages, acronyms, spellings, etc., and explanatory references, are made by more experienced catalogers.

Exercises

Do the descriptive cataloging for the items listed below. Choose the main entry/ access points and list added entry/access points in the tracing. Do not add subject headings; these will be discussed in the next chapter. Answers to these exercises can be found in the Appendix.

Exercise 4A: Do a first level and a second level bibliographic record for the book pictured in Exercise 4A using the traditional bibliographic style.

This book is 29 cm. in height, is mostly photographs, and has 168 pages of text.

Note: Do the publication/distribution statement in a way appropriate for a U.S or a Canadian library.

(title page)

EThIOPIA
PHOTOGRAPHED
HISTORIC PHOTOGRAPHS OF THE COUNTRY
AND ITS PEOPLE TAKEN BETWEEN
1867 AND 1935

RICHARD PANKHURST
&
DENIS GÉRARD

KEGAN PAUL INTERNATIONAL
LONDON AND NEW YORK

(information on verso)

First published in 1996 by
Kegan Paul International
UK: P.O. Box 256, London WC1B 3SW, England
Tel: (0171) 580 5511 Fax: (0171) 436 0899
E-mail: books@keganpau.demon.co.uk
Internet: http://www.demon.co.uk/keganpaul/
USA: 562 West 113th Street, New York, NY, 10025, USA
Tel: (212) 666 1000 Fax: (212) 316 3100

Distributed by
John Wiley & Sons Ltd
Southern Cross Trading Estate
1 Oldlands Way, Bognor Regis
West Sussex, PO22 9SA, England
Tel: (01243) 779 777 Fax: (01243) 820 250

Columbia University Press
562 West 113th Street
New York, NY 10025. USA
Tel: (212) 666 1000 Fax: (212) 316 3100

Set in Korinna Medium
Printed in Great Britain by T.J. Press, Padstow, Cornwall

British Library Cataloguing in Publication Data

Pankhurst, Richard, 1927 –
Ethiopia photographed: historic photographs of the country and its people
taken between 1867 and 1935
1. Ethiopians – Portraits 2. Ethiopians – Pictorial works
3. Ethiopia – Social life and customs – Pictorial works
I. Title II. Gérard, Denis
963'.04'0222
ISBN 0-7103-0504-4

Library of Congress Cataloging-in-Publication Data
Applied for

Exercise 4B: Do a first level and a second level bibliographic record for the book pictured below as Exercise 4B using the traditional bibliographic style.

This book is 23 cm. in height, has no illustrations, and has 259 pages of text and xix preliminary pages.

(title page)

Cross-Cultural Perspectives on Knowledge Management

Edited by David J. Pauleen

Libraries Unlimited Knowledge Management Series
Danny Wallace, Series Editor

U N L I M I T E D
A Member of the Greenwood Publishing Group

Westport, Connecticut • London

(information on verso)

Library of Congress Cataloging-in-Publication Data

Cross-cultural perspectives on knowledge management / edited by David J. Pauleen.
    p. cm. — (Libraries Unlimited knowledge management series)
    Includes bibliographical references and index.
    ISBN 1–59158–331–4 (alk. paper)
    1. Knowledge management.   2. Corporate culture.   I. Pauleen, David, 1957–
    HD30.2.C78   2007
    658.4′038—dc22   2006028274

British Library Cataloguing in Publication Data is available.

Library of Congress Catalog Card Number: 2006028274
ISBN: 1–59158–331–4

First published in 2007

Libraries Unlimited, 88 Post Road West, Westport, CT 06881
A Member of the Greenwood Publishing Group, Inc.
www.lu.com

Printed in the United States of America

The paper used in this book complies with the
Permanent Paper Standard issued by the National
Information Standards Organization (Z39.48–1984).

10 9 8 7 6 5 4 3 2 1

Exercise 4C: Do the descriptive cataloging for a first level and a second level record using the traditional bibliographic style for the book pictured below as Exercise 4C. It has no CIP.

This book is 24 cm. in height, has general illustrations, and has 189 pages of text and xiii preliminary pages.

(title page)

LIFE SIGNS

THE BIOLOGY OF STAR TREK

**SUSAN JENKINS, M.D., and
ROBERT JENKINS, M.D., PH.D.**

Foreword by Lawrence M. Krauss, Ph.D.,
author of *The Physics of Star Trek*

HarperCollins*Publishers*

(information on verso)

Illustration on page 107 reprinted with permission of Scribner, a division of Simon & Schuster, from The Double Helix by James D. Watson. Copyright © 1968 by James D. Watson.

LIFE SIGNS—THE BIOLOGY OF STAR TREK. Copyright © 1998 by Robert Jenkins and Susan Jenkins. All rights reserved. Printed in the United States of America. No part of this book may be used or reproduced in any manner whatsoever without written permission except in the case of brief quotations embodied in critical articles and reviews. For information address HarperCollins Publishers, Inc., 10 East 53rd Street, New York, NY 10022.

HarperCollins books may be purchased for educational, business, or sales promotional use. For information please write: Special Markets Department, HarperCollins Publishers, Inc., 10 East 53rd Street, New York, NY 10022.

FIRST EDITION

Designed by Elliott Beard

ISBN 0-06-019154-6

98 99 00 01 02 ❖ / RRD 10 9 8 7 6 5 4 3 2 1

Exercise 4D: This is a more challenging exercise. In choosing the main entry/access point, consider who is responsible for the intellectual content of the work. If this book were in a library with a large collection of works by and about Shaw, a uniform title may be wanted. Make a guess what the uniform title might be.

Do two bibliographic descriptions at the second level of description—one with a uniform title and one without a uniform title. There is no CIP.

This book is 20 cm. in height, has no illustrations, and has 64 pages of text.

(title page)

The Sayings of

BERNARD
SHAW

edited by

Joseph Spence

(information on verso)

This impression 2002
First published in 1993 by
Gerald Duckworth & Co. Ltd.
61 Frith Street, London W1D 3JL
Tel: 020 7434 4242
Fax: 020 7434 4420
inquiries@duckworth-publishers.co.uk
www.ducknet.co.uk

Quotations from the works of Bernard Shaw
© 1993 by The Trustees of the British Museum,
the Governors and Guardians of the National
Gallery of Ireland and Royal Academy
of Dramatic Art

Introduction and editorial arrangement
© 1993 by Joseph Spence

All rights reserved. No part of this publication
may be reproduced, stored in a retrieval system, or
transmitted, in any form or by any means, electronic,
mechanical, photocopying, recording or otherwise,
without the prior permission of the publisher.

A catalogue record for this book is available
from the British Library

ISBN 0 7156 2491 1

Duckworth

Printed in Great Britain by
Antony Rowe Ltd, Eastbourne

Additional Information

5

Subject Headings

Half the job of cataloging is to identify and describe a book—called *descriptive cataloging*—explained in the last two chapters. The rest of the job is identifying and describing its contents. In a process called *subject analysis*, catalogers determine what the book is about and assign subject headings that serve as access points, which are listed alphabetically in the catalog along with the headings described in Chapter 4. Call numbers, which are also given in catalog records and reflect subject matter, will be discussed in Chapter 6.

Two standard subject heading lists are normally used for general collections in the English-speaking world: *Sears List of Subject Headings* (Sears) and *Library of Congress Subject Headings* (LCSH). (Specialized lists for use with subject specific collections are not discussed in this book.) Sears and LCSH are lists of authorized subject headings that have been predetermined along with other words and phrases designated as cross-references.

Sears and LCSH: A Comparison

Publication

Sears headings are found in one volume totalling more than 800 pages, while LCSH is published in five very large oversized volumes. Sears is designed for small and medium-sized collections (20,000 volumes is the recommended collection size limit for users of Sears), while LCSH is designed for large collections, research collections, and for libraries that have holdings in narrowly defined subject areas.

Sears is published every few years; the present nineteenth edition appeared just three years after the eighteenth edition, the shortest period between editions since this work was first published in 1923. It is also available online as a WilsonWeb database, which contains new headings that have been added since the publication of the nineteenth edition in 2007. LCSH is published every year and is also available in an electronic format. Access to the electronic version, part of *Classification Web*, which is updated continuously, is available by subscription from LC's Cataloging Distribution Service. A list of subject authorities is also available free of charge on the World Wide Web at http://authorities.loc.gov/. It includes name, name-title, and series titles, as well as topical subject authority records.

Assistance in Understanding

In its preliminary pages, Sears provides "Principles of the Sears List" (pages xv–xxxix), an introduction to subject analysis that should be read by all students and beginning catalogers. Sears' explanation of subject headings is written in clear English and is an excellent description of the function and construction of subject headings. Catalogers who assign Library of Congress subject headings can easily adapt the "Principles of the Sears List" to refer to the LC subject list because the fundamental principles of subject analysis are the same.

The Library of Congress publishes a separate *Subject Cataloging Manual: Subject Headings* (SCMSH), which provides the most complete guidance in applying LCSH. SCMSH consists of a series of policy statements covering topics of interest to subject catalogers using LCSH as their subject heading list, such as how to propose new subject headings, how subdivisions should be assigned, and how to treat nonbook materials, selected genres of literature, and selected topical areas. SCMSH is available by subscription from the Library of Congress's Cataloging Distribution Service in print as a loose-leaf publication or online as part of *Cataloger's Desktop*. Instructions in SCMSH tend to be specific. They may expand on general instructions found in the prefatory material and the helpful scope notes given under some headings in LCSH or provide instructions when none are present in LCSH.

Terminology

Sears is a list of subject terms created by Sears' editors with the help of its editorial board. While it does not possess all the features of a true thesaurus, it shows some of the relationships among the terms it authorizes for use as subject headings. This is also true of LCSH. Terms in both Sears and LCSH are created when the cataloging of current sources of information reveal a need for them. Terms are based on what is known as "literary warrant," that is, the existence of *literature* on a subject *warrants* the addition of a term to the subject heading list.

An important difference between Sears and LCSH is that Sears' terminology is simpler and less sophisticated than LCSH's. Sears employs terminology that tends to be broad in meaning, nontechnical, and understandable to nonspecialists. For example, two LCSH headings (**Science -- Philosophy** and **Complexity (Philosophy)**) have been assigned in the CIP of a book titled *Complexity: The Emerging Science at the Edge of Order and Chaos*. The Sears list does not have the second subject heading. This second LCSH heading is suited to a library that has a large collection of items on the philosophies related to science, while in a much smaller, less academic collection, the heading **Science -- Philosophy** would be adequate.

Sears often has one term for a topical area while LCSH uses more than one, distinguishing finer differences within the area. For example, Sears uses "**Aquatic animals**," while LCSH uses "**Aquatic animals**," "**Aquatic insects**," "**Aquatic invertebrates**," "**Aquatic mammals**," "**Aquatic organisms**," "**Aquatic pests**," "**Aquatic reptiles**," and "**Aquatic warblers**." Another example: Sears uses "**Cooking**," while LCSH uses "**Cookery**" and has many more headings beginning with the word "Cookery." A third example: Sears uses "**Conferences**," while LCSH uses four different terms for this concept: "**Clergy conferences**," "**Congresses and conventions**," "**Forums (Discussion and debate)**," and "**Meetings**."

Number of Subject Headings Assigned

The CIPs in the figures and exercises in this book demonstrate a range in the number of subject headings that are assigned to an item. In the past, when cards had to be filed by hand in card catalogs, it was important to cut down on the amount of filing work by minimizing the number of subject headings and another type of the Rule of Three (in addition to the one described in Chapter 3) prevailed. It mandated that no more than three subject headings be assigned to a book. If a book covered four distinct subjects, a broader subject heading was to be assigned that included all of them. Later, the Library of Congress expanded its subject heading assignments to a new rule called the "Twenty Percent Rule," which mandated a subject heading for a subject if it comprised at least twenty percent of a book's content. Currently, the Twenty Percent Rule has been relaxed, and subject catalogers are encouraged to assign as many subject headings as they believe will prove useful to searchers. (An example of multiple subject headings is found in Figure 5.6 on page 74). Sears, however, still recommends the Rule of Three and states that more than three subject headings should be assigned only after careful consideration, and that a subject heading should not be assigned for a topic that comprises less than one-third of a book. Beginning catalogers should follow a library's policy about the number of subject headings assigned.

Alphabetizing

The alphabetizing of subject heading lists has also changed with the advent of computerized cataloging. When card catalogs were the norm, a human filer was able to treat digits and abbreviations as if they were the spelled-out words. The abbreviation "Dr." was filed as if it was the whole word "Doctor," digits such as "10" were filed as if they were the word "ten," and all forms of the prefix "Mc" and "Mac" in names were filed as if they were spelled "Mac."

Two different methods of alphabetizing subject headings have since been developed and are used in Sears and LCSH and the catalogs that employ them. The first, titled *ALA Filing Rules*, is sponsored by the American Library Association and is used to arrange the headings in *Sears List of Subject Headings*. The second, titled *Library of Congress Filing Rules*, is sponsored by the Library of Congress and is used to arrange headings in LCSH. Both sets of rules mandate treating digits as digits, preceding the alphabetic characters and arranged in numeric value order: 1, 2, 15, 103, 1364, etc. Both sets of rules accept abbreviations "as is" and file them the way they appear. The principal difference between ALA and LC filing rules is the way they accommodate different kinds of punctuation and the way they handle subdivisions. The ALA rules ignore all punctuation, filing the entire string of words in a subject heading word by word regardless of the punctuation that separates them, including the long dashes that indicate subdivision. In contrast, the LC rules mandate recognizing punctuation within headings and filing headings with commas differently than headings with parentheses, etc., and filing subdivisions of different types in order: chronological subdivisions first, topical subdivisions second, and geographic subdivisions last. Figures 5.1 and 5.2 illustrate the differences.

FIGURE 5.1   Headings Filed Using ALA Filing Rules (1980), Used by Sears

Music -- Acoustics and physics

Music and literature

Music appreciation

Music -- Discography

Music festivals

Music, Gospel USE Gospel music

Music -- History and criticism

Music -- Psychological aspects

FIGURE 5.2   Headings Filed Using LC Filing Rules (1980), Used by LCSH

Music -- Acoustics and physics

Music -- Discography

Music -- History and criticism

Music -- Psychological aspects

Music, Gospel USE Gospel music

Music and literature

Music appreciation

Music festivals

Format

The presentation of subject headings in the print versions of Sears and LCSH have a similar format, as demonstrated in Figures 5.3 and 5.4. Students can readily transfer the skills learned in using one of these subject heading lists if they are required to use the other.

In Sears, authorized headings are always printed in boldface type wherever they appear. In LCSH, authorized headings are printed in boldface type as part of the main list, but not where they appear as headings in cross-references.

Roman print is used for cross-references that are not authorized for use in Sears and LCSH. It is easy to distinguish between authorized terms and unauthorized cross-references because of this practice. Subdivided headings that are authorized for use, such as **Civil rights—Codification** (in Figure 5.4), appear entirely in boldface type.

Civil rights is an authorized heading in both the Sears and LCSH lists. The heading is followed by "(May subdiv. geog.)" in Sears and "(May Subd. Geog)" in LCSH, which means that a geographic name may be added to the subject heading. (The difference in practice between Sears' direct and LCSH's indirect geographic subdivisions is explained on the next page and illustrated in Figure 5.5.)

Next comes classification numbers: from the fourteenth abridged edition of the *Dewey Decimal Classification and Relative Index* for Sears and from the Library of Congress classification for LCSH. Many subject headings have only one classification number. In Figures 5.3 and 5.4, there are two classification numbers for **Civil rights** that can be applied depending on the orientation of the book being cataloged. LCSH provides some help in determining which volume of the Library of Congress classification should be consulted. Sears does not need to do this because the *Abridged Dewey Decimal Classification and Relative Index* is contained in one volume. (323 covers civil and political rights and 342 constitutional and administrative law.) Classification numbers will be discussed in Chapter 6.

Both Sears and LCSH have a scope note for **Civil rights** that details its use. Not all authorized headings need a scope note. The UF, SA, BT, NT, and RT references will be explained later in this chapter under the section titled "Subject Cross-References."

Sears and LCSH do not list all potential authorized headings; instead, catalogers are instructed at some headings to add more specific terms if they need them. For example, the kinds of headings that may be added by the cataloger as needed include common things such as foods, sports, plants and animals, chemicals and minerals, enterprises and industries, diseases, organs and regions of the body, languages, ethnic groups and nationalities, wars and battles, and the names of people, geographic names, and corporate bodies. Sears also provides a list of " 'Key' Headings" (p. xli), which serve as patterns for the development of similar subject headings, for example, **Shakespeare, William** for other voluminous authors and **Presidents—United States** for public figures in any country.

Subdivision Use

The difference in the level of subdivision use between Sears and LCSH is both clear and logical. A small collection indexed using Sears is unlikely to need or want many subdivisions to express the contents of its materials. If many narrowly defined headings were used, individual headings could apply to so few items that very little collocation would occur and searching by subject under such a system would retrieve only one or two items. Sears provides a list of more than 300 topical subdivisions used within the list. These are listed on six pages preceding the main list of headings.

Large collections, on the other hand, need the much more specific and numerous subject headings found in the first volume of the printed edition of LCSH, which furnishes more than 3,500 authorized subdivisions consisting of general terms called "free-floating" subdivisions and rules for their assignment. This list of free-floating subdivisions is available from the Library of Congress Cataloging Distribution Service by subscription as a printed loose-leaf publication updated twice a year or online as part of both *Cataloger's Desktop* and *Classification Web*.

As mentioned above, in both Sears and LCSH, a direction in parenthesis "(May subdiv. geog.)" following a subject heading indicates that a geographic location may be added to the subject heading. However, Sears uses direct subdivisions and LCSH employs indirect subdivisions. Figure 5.5 shows the different displays that result from direct and indirect geographic subdivision practice.

Classification Numbers

Both Sears and LCSH provide an appropriate classification number(s) for most subject headings as mentioned above in the section titled "Format." See Chapter 6 for a discussion of classification.

LCSH Printed Versus Online Edition

If a beginning cataloger does not have the print edition of LCSH available, it is necessary to access the online version at http://authorities.loc.gov/ to check or select LC subject headings. The following steps are necessary to access any subject heading. For example, to access **Civil rights**, you must do the following:

(1) Go to http://authorities.loc.gov/ and select "Search Authorities."
(2) In the next screen, type "civil rights" in the search text box. Click "Begin Search."
(3) A red box appearing to the left of the subject heading indicates this as an authorized heading; click it.
(4) In the next screen, select "Authority Record."
(5) In the next screen, select "Civil rights."
(6) In the next screen, which displays the MARC coded record for "Civil rights," select "Labelled Display."
(7) The final screen provides the same UF, BT, RT, and SA references as the print edition, but not the NT references.

FIGURE 5.3   Sears List of Subject Headings

Civil engineering—*Continued*
    Dams
    Drainage
    Dredging
    Excavation
    Extraterrestrial bases
    Harbors
    Highway engineering
    Hydraulic engineering
    Lunar bases
    Marine engineering
    Mechanical engineering
    Military engineering
    Mining engineering
    Public works
    Railroad engineering
    Reclamation of land
    Roads
    Streets
    Structural engineering
    Structural steel
    Surveying
    Tunnels
    Walls
    Water supply engineering
Civil government
  USE   **Political science**
Civil law suits
  USE   **Litigation**
Civil liberty
  USE   **Freedom**
Civil procedure (May subdiv. geog.)
    347
  BT   **Courts**
  NT   **Probate law and practice**
      Small claims courts
  RT   **Litigation**
Civil rights (May subdiv. geog.)   **323;**
    342

    Use for materials on citizens' rights as established by law or protected by a constitution. Materials on the rights of persons regardless of their legal, socioeconomic, or cultural status and as recognized by the international community are entered under **Human rights**.

  UF   Basic rights
      Constitutional rights
      Fundamental rights
  SA   ethnic groups and classes of persons with the subdivision *Civil rights* [to be added as needed]

  BT   **Constitutional law**
      Human rights
      Political science
  NT   **African Americans—Civil rights**
      Anti-apartheid movement
      Blacks—Civil rights
      Children—Civil rights
      Due process of law
      Employee rights
      Fair trial
      Freedom of assembly
      Freedom of association
      Freedom of information
      Freedom of movement
      Freedom of religion
      Freedom of speech
      Freedom of the press
      Gay rights
      Habeas corpus
      Right of privacy
      Right of property
      Women's rights
  RT   **Civil rights demonstrations**
      Discrimination
      Freedom
Civil rights demonstrations (May subdiv. geog.)   **322.4**
  UF   Demonstrations for civil rights
      Freedom marches for civil rights
      Marches for civil rights
      Sit-ins for civil rights
  BT   **Demonstrations**
  RT   **Civil rights**
Civil rights (International law)
  USE   **Human rights**
Civil servants
  USE   **Civil service**
Civil service (May subdiv. geog.)   **351;**
    352.6; 342

    Use for general materials on career government service and the laws governing it. Materials on civil service employees are entered under the name of the country, state, city, corporate body, or government agency with the subdivision *Officials and employees*.

  UF   Administration
      Civil servants
      Employees and officials
      Government employees
      Government service
      Officials and employees
      Tenure of office

FIGURE 5.4   Library of Congress List of Subject Headings

Civil rights   *(May Subd Geog)*
  [JC571-JC628 *(Political science)*]
  [K3236-K3268 *(Law)*]
  Here are entered works on citizens' rights as established by law and protected by constitution. Works on the rights of persons regardless of their legal, socioeconomic or cultural status and as recognized by the international community are entered under Human rights.
  UF Basic rights
      Civil liberties
      Constitutional rights
      Fundamental rights
      Rights, Civil
  BT Constitutional law
      Human rights
  RT Political persecution
  SA *subdivision* Civil rights *under classes of persons and ethnic groups*
  NT Discrimination—Law and legislation
      Due process of law
      Employee rights
      Equality before the law
      Free choice of employment
      Freedom of association
      Freedom of expression
      Freedom of information
      Freedom of movement
      Freedom of speech
      Gay rights
      Habeas corpus
      Indians of North America—Civil rights
      Indigenous peoples—Civil rights
      Political rights
      Privacy, Right of
      Right of property
      Right to education
      Speedy trial
      State action (Civil rights)
  —**Codification**
  —**Religious aspects**
      [BL65.C58]
  ——**Baptists, [Catholic Church, etc.]**
  ——**Buddhism, [Christianity, etc.]**
  ——**Catholic Church**
      UF Civil rights (Canon law)
          [Former heading]
  ——**Christianity**
      UF Church and civil rights
          [Former heading]
          Civil rights (Christian theology)
          [Former heading]
      BT Liberation theology
  —**United States**
Civil rights (Canon law)
  USE Civil rights—Religious aspects—
       Catholic Church
       Human rights—Religious aspects—
       Catholic Church
Civil rights (Christian theology)
  USE Civil rights—Religious aspects—
       Christianity
Civil rights (International law)
  USE Human rights
Civil rights (Islamic law)   *(May Subd Geog)*
  BT Islamic law
Civil rights (Jewish law)
  BT Jewish law
Civil rights activists
  USE Civil rights workers
Civil rights and communism
  USE Civil rights and socialism
Civil rights and socialism   *(May Subd Geog)*
  [HX550.C58]
  UF Civil rights and communism
      Communism and civil rights
  BT Socialism

Civil rights demonstrations   *(May Subd Geog)*
  UF Freedom marches (Civil rights)
      Sit-ins (Civil rights)
  BT Civil rights movements
      Demonstrations
  —**Alabama**
      NT Montgomery Bus Boycott,
          Montgomery, Ala., 1955-1956
          Selma-Montgomery Rights March,
          1965
  —**Northern Ireland**
      NT Bloody Sunday, Derry, Northern
          Ireland, 1972
  —**United States**
      NT Trail of Broken Treaties, 1972
  —**Washington (D.C.)**
      NT March on Washington for Jobs and
          Freedom, Washington, D.C.,
          1963
          National March on Washington
          for Lesbian and Gay Rights,
          Washington, D.C., 1979
          National March on Washington
          for Lesbian and Gay Rights,
          Washington, D.C., 1987
Civil rights in art   *(Not Subd Geog)*
Civil rights in literature   *(Not Subd Geog)*
Civil Rights Memorial (Montgomery, Ala.)
  BT Memorials—Alabama
Civil rights movements   *(May Subd Geog)*
  UF Civil liberation movements
      Liberation movements (Civil rights)
      Protest movements (Civil rights)
  BT Human rights movements
  NT Anti-apartheid movements
      Civil rights demonstrations
  —**United States**
      NT Chicano movement
Civil rights movements in art
  (Not Subd Geog)
Civil rights movements in literature
  (Not Subd Geog)
Civil rights workers   *(May Subd Geog)*
  UF Civil rights activists
      Race relations reformers
  BT Social reformers
  NT Anti-apartheid activists
      Women civil rights workers
  —**United States**
      NT African American civil rights
          workers
Civil rights workers, African American
  USE African American civil rights workers
Civil rights workers, Black   *(May Subd Geog)*
  UF Black civil rights workers
Civil rights workers in literature
  (Not Subd Geog)
Civil servants
  USE *subdivision* Officials and employees
       *under names of countries, cities,
       etc., e.g.* United States—Officials
       and employees; *and subdivision*
       Government employees *under specific
       subjects, e.g.* Collective bargaining—
       Government employees; Collective
       labor agreements—Government
       employees
       Civil service
Civil service   *(May Subd Geog)*
  [JF1601-JF1674]
  Here are entered works on career government service and the laws governing it. Works on government service, including that by political appointment or employment contract, are entered under the name of the country, state, or city, with the subdivision Officials and employees. Works on personnel of a specific government agency are entered under the name of that agency, with the subdivision Officials and employees.
  Works on public sector employment as a countercyclical policy measure intended to provide jobs for the unemployed as well as to provide economic assistance to distressed areas and state and local government are entered under Public service employment.

  UF Bureaucrats
      Career government service
      Civil servants
      Civil service—Law and legislation
      Civil service—Legal status, laws, etc.
      Government employees
      Government service
      Public employees
      Public service (Civil service)
  BT Public administration
  RT Public officers
      Public service employment
  NT Anthropologists in government
      Applications for office
      Architects in government
      Budget analysts
      Civil list
      Civil service, Colonial
      Criminal justice personnel
      Disabled veterans in the civil service
      Employee-management relations in
      government
      Engineers in government
      Gays in the civil service
      Government business enterprises—
      Employees
      Intergovernmental personnel programs
      Local officials and employees
      Municipal officials and employees
      People with disabilities in the civil
      service
      Political scientists in government
      Professional employees in government
      Psychologists in government
      Scientists in government
      Social scientists in government
      Women in the civil service
  —**Awards**   *(May Subd Geog)*
  ——**United States**
      NT Rockefeller Public Service
          Awards
  —Collective bargaining
      USE Collective bargaining—
           Government employees
  —Collective labor agreements
      USE Collective labor agreements—
           Government employees
  —Colonies
      USE Civil service, Colonial
  —Ethics
      USE Civil service ethics
  —**Examinations**
      [JK716 *(United States)*]
      UF Civil service examinations
          Competitive examinations
      BT Examinations
  —**Furloughs**   *(Not Subd Geog)*
      Here are entered works on the placement of civil servants in a temporary status without duties and pay because of lack of work or funds or other nondisciplinary reasons. Works limited to particular localities are entered under the name of the country, city, etc., with subdivision Officials and employees—Furloughs. Works limited to specific departments or agencies are entered under the name of the department or agency, with subdivision Officials and employees—Furloughs.
      UF Civil service furloughs
          Furloughs
      BT Layoff systems
      SA *subdivision* Officials and
          employees—Furloughs *under
          names of countries, cities, etc.;
          and under names of individual
          government departments,
          agencies, etc.*
  —**Labor productivity**   *(May Subd Geog)*
      BT Government productivity
  —Labor unions
      USE Government employee unions

1462

FIGURE 5.5   Direct and Indirect Geographic Subdivision

SUBDIVIDED DIRECTLY (SEARS)	SUBDIVIDED INDIRECTLY (LCSH)
Education -- Atlanta (Ga.)	Education -- Canada
Education -- Buffalo (N.Y.)	Education -- France
Education -- Canada	Education -- France -- Paris
Education -- France	Education -- Georgia -- Atlanta
Education -- New York (State)	Education -- New York (State)
Education -- Ontario	Education -- New York (State) -- Buffalo
Education -- Paris	Education -- Ontario
Education -- Toronto (Ont.)	Education -- Ontario -- Toronto

In order to access the NT references, click "Next" near the bottom of the screen, which will lead you to the first NT reference in the print version, "Discrimination Law and legislation." Clicking "Next" at the bottom of this screen will lead to "Due process of law," and clicking "Next" on each screen in turn will bring up all the NT references in the print version.

A comparison of the two versions shows that the printed version of LCSH seems to be easier for beginning catalogers to use than the online version because it is possible to consider many subject heading possibilities on one page, while in the online version a cataloger must access a number of files to gain the same information.

CIP Records and Subject Headings

Most CIP records provide subject headings derived from the list used by the agency that has done the cataloging. For example, Library of Congress CIPs have LCSH headings, and Library and Archives of Canada CIPs have LCSH headings modified by *Canadian Subject Headings*, which are described later in this chapter. If the library uses LCSH, all subject headings found in CIPs should be checked, the only exceptions being books that are published in the same year in which the cataloging is being done. The reason for this checking is because a new edition of LCSH is published each year with new and changed subject headings and the electronic version of LCSH is updated regularly. Popular terminology changes over time, for example, negroes to black Americans to **African Americans**, or new subject matter appears that requires the development of a heading, for example, **iPod (Digital music player)**, or a subject heading that needs qualification to distinguish it from the same term with a different meaning, for example, **Mice** and **Mice (Computers)**. If a beginning cataloger finds a subject heading that has changed from the one presently found in the library's catalog, she or he should give this record to an experienced cataloger, who will make a decision about which form of the subject heading to use.

If a library uses Sears, all subject headings in the CIPs must be checked in the Sears list. Many of the Sears headings are the same as those in LCSH. However, some will need to be changed. For example, Sears uses **Map drawing** while LCSH includes both **Cartography** and **Map drawing** with a note to indicate that **Map drawing** is only applied to the mapping of small areas. Exercise 5A at the end of this chapter provides experience in adapting tracings using LCSH to Sears.

Sometimes, the subject headings in the CIP record are incorrect. It is possible that the publisher did not give the cataloging agency enough information to correctly identify a work's intellectual content. Publishers send this information well ahead of the publishing date and sometimes material has been changed before the publication date. Beginning catalogers should give books that cause any concern about the appropriateness of a subject heading to an experienced cataloger.

Choosing Subject Headings

A library will receive some books that do not have CIPs, or the CIP does not include subject headings (see the CIP in Figure 2.2 on page 7), and catalogers will need to assign subject headings. In general, the rules for choosing subject headings are as follows:

1. Determine the subject(s) of the item being cataloged by examining its subject-rich elements (title, table of contents, preface, introduction, summary, index, and book jacket), considering these from a user's viewpoint.

2. Write the subject(s) down in your own words.

3. Match each subject listed with the headings in Sears or LCSH, assigning the heading authorized for use that most closely represents it.

4. For Sears, assign up to three subject headings per item. If an item covers more than three subjects, assign a broader heading that includes them. For example, if a book is about cattle, sheep, and pigs on a farm, assign three headings: **Cattle**; **Sheep**; **Pigs** (**Swine**, if using LCSH). If it covers cattle, sheep, pigs, and horses, assign **Domestic animals**. For LCSH, assign as many subject headings per item as are needed to represent its contents accurately.

5. Choose the most specific heading available, not a broader heading.

6. Give the most specific authorized heading available directly, not as a subdivision of a broader heading.

7. Consider items already in the collection relating to the subject of the item being cataloged and try to collocate it with existing holdings on the same subject.

8. Treat items first by topic, then by geographical focus or by form, unless Sears' or LCSH's scope notes instruct doing otherwise.

9. Read "Principles of the Sears List" or consult LC's *Subject Cataloging Manual: Subject Headings* for help in assigning subject headings.

If a satisfactory subject heading has not been found at the end of this process, as sometimes happens with a book about complex subjects or subjects outside the beginning cataloger's knowledge, the descriptive cataloging part of the record should be given to an experienced cataloger for subject analysis.

Following the nine steps listed above does not mean that every cataloger in every library will end up choosing the same subject heading(s) for a particular book. This is demonstrated by the subject headings in the CIPs in Figure 2.3 on page 8 chosen by catalogers in two prestigious libraries. While both acknowledge this book as an autobiography of Oliver Sacks, the Library of Congress also has the additional subject heading **Neurologists -- England -- Biography**, which allows the book to be listed with other materials on the subject of neurologists and neurology. The National Library of Canada (that is, the Library and Archives of Canada) treats this book purely as a biography because it is about Sacks' boyhood, not his years as a neurologist.

Subject Cross-References

Cross-references expand the vocabulary of the subject catalog and make it possible for searchers to find materials even when they are unaware of the authorized subject headings being used. This contributes to the user-friendliness of the catalog and adds desirable flexibility without losing the gathering function of a controlled vocabulary.

The examples in the explanation of cross-references below refer to Figures 5.3 and 5.4 on pages 68 and 69. Note that LCSH has a larger number of references because it has a much larger number of authorized headings. Some of the references in the Sears list might be missing in the LCSH list because they may be authorized headings in the LCSH list.

USE reference leads someone from an unauthorized term to the authorized heading. For example, the unauthorized phrase "Civil servants" is followed by a USE reference that says, "USE **Civil service**" in both lists and additional suggestions about subdivisions in the LCSH list.

UF (Use For). An example is the UF reference at **Civil rights** that tells the cataloger to use this term in place of "Constitutional rights." Every USE reference generates a reciprocal UF reference under the authorized heading.

BT (Broader Term) listed under a subject heading will give headings at the next broader level of subject specificity. BT references always generate NT reciprocals. For example, the subject heading **Civil rights** lists **Constitutional law** as one of its BTs.

NT (Narrower Term) listed under a subject heading will give headings at the next narrower level. For example, the subject heading **Civil rights** lists **Freedom of information** as one of its NTs.

RT (Related Term) also indicates subject relationships, but at more-or-less equivalent levels of specificity. RTs always generate RT reciprocals with the terms they reference. Sometimes RTs are similar to one another in meaning and other times they are opposites. For example, the RTs in the Sears list, **Civil rights** and **Freedom,** mean similar things, while the RTs **Civil rights** and **Discrimination** have opposite but related meanings.

SA (See Also) are references to groups of headings, not individual headings. They may tell catalogers to establish new headings of a certain kind, to use the heading word or phrase in a particular pattern, or to use it as a subdivision under selected types of main headings. For example, the SA under **Civil rights** suggests using this term as a subdivision with ethnic groups and classes of persons, such as in **Children -- Civil rights** listed in Sears as an NT.

Blind references. One of the most aggravating things for a catalog user is a reference to a subject heading, personal name, or corporate name that does not exist in the catalog. This is called a blind reference. For example, if all the books about the civil service have been weeded or lost from a collection, the direction "Civil servants USE Civil service" should be removed from the catalog. Some OPACs are coded to do this automatically.

Subject Headings for Literary Works

Until the latter part of the twentieth century, North American subject cataloging practice was to omit subject headings for individual literary works, such as novels, plays, poetry, and the like. In part, this may have been because works of imagination are not "true," or it may have been a practical way of cutting down the job of original subject cataloging, or it may have been based on the assumption that members of the public search literary works by author and/or title. However, this view of cataloging has changed over the last several decades. Subject headings are routinely applied to many literary works.

It is not difficult to assign subject headings to novels. The subdivision "Fiction" is added to the appropriate subject heading for both Sears and LCSH (see Figure 5.6). Page xxx in Sears provides a list of nine guidelines that should be read before assigning fiction subject headings. *Guidelines on Subject Access to Individual Works of Fiction, Drama, Etc.*, which is oriented to LCSH, is another useful subject cataloging tool.

LC's Annotated Card Program

The list of more than 950 Annotated Card (AC) Program headings appears at the beginning of the first volume of LCSH, along with a brief history of the initiative and brief descriptions of the categories of headings, application policies, subdivisions, references, scope notes, and AC products. These headings can also be found in *Classification Web*.

The Library of Congress developed the Annotated Card Program in the 1960s. Subject headings suited to children's materials—both fiction as well as nonfiction—and summaries of the contents of a book were added to catalog records prepared by LC's children's materials cataloging staff. AC cataloging for materials designated for young readers was given the following variant treatments:

1. Subdivisions indicating age levels, such as **—Juvenile literature**, were dropped (see Figure 5.8 on page 78).

2. Subject headings were added, revised, or simplified to make them more appropriate to children's vocabularies and children's materials.

3. Subdivision practice was modified to give subject access to individual works of fiction and to biographies in fields where LCSH had no established term for persons in that field. (The reasoning was that children learn as much from fiction as from nonfiction.)

4. Summaries were provided in the descriptive cataloging.

In the CIP records found on the verso of a children's book, the headings are enclosed in square brackets. For example, in Figure 5.7, the square brackets around "[1. Fairy tales. 2. Mice—Fiction]" indicate that these are AC headings.

Sometimes, books suitable for children are acquired for an adult collection, such as an education library. Catalog records for these books would be given the subdivision "—Juvenile drama," "—Juvenile fiction," "—Juvenile literature," or "—Juvenile poetry." In Figure 5.8, the CIP shows both adult and the AC subject headings.

FIGURE 5.6

This example is an illustration of:
- fiction book
- ISBNs with qualifications for different formats
- comparison of Sears and Library of Congress subject headings
- title added entry
- Library of Congress CIP
- two levels of cataloging

1st level cataloging with Sears subject headings

Lewycka, Marina.
  A short history of tractors in Ukranian. -- Penguin Books, 2006.
  294 p.

  ISBN 0-1430-3674-2 (pbk).

  1. Ukranians -- Great Britain -- Fiction. 2. Children of immigrants
-- Fiction. 3. Parents -- Fiction. 4. Young women -- Fiction.
5. Elderly -- Fiction. 6. Widowers -- Fiction. 7. Sisters -- Fiction.
I. Title.

2nd level cataloging with Library of Congress subject headings

Lewycka, Marina.
  A short history of tractors in Ukranian / Marina Lewycka. -- New York
: Penguin Books, 2006.
  294 p. ; 24 cm.

  ISBN 1-59420-044-0 (hardcover).

  1. Ukranians -- Great Britain -- Fiction. 2. Children of immigrants
-- Fiction. 3. Older parents -- Fiction. 4. Young women -- Fiction.
5. Older men -- Fiction. 6. Widowers -- Fiction. 7. Sisters --
Fiction. I. Title.

**The publication/distribution area in a second level description for
a Canadian catalog would read:**

New York ; Toronto : Penguin Books, 2006.

Fig. 5.6—Continues

The Canadian Connection

Both Sears and LCSH have companion lists of subject headings for materials with Canadian content suitable for use by Canadian catalogers and those catalogers working with significant collections of Canadian materials in U.S. libraries.

FIGURE 5.6 *(continued)*

(title page)

a short history
of
tractors
in ukrainian

MARINA LEWYCKA

PENGUIN BOOKS

(information on verso)

PENGUIN BOOKS
Published by the Penguin Group
Penguin Group (USA) Inc., 375 Hudson Street, New York, New York 10014, U.S.A.
Penguin Group (Canada), 90 Eglinton Avenue East, Suite 700, Toronto,
Ontario, Canada M4P 2Y3 (a division of Pearson Penguin Canada Inc.)
Penguin Books Ltd, 80 Strand, London WC2R 0RL, England
Penguin Ireland, 25 St Stephen's Green, Dublin 2, Ireland (a division of Penguin Books Ltd)
Penguin Group (Australia), 250 Camberwell Road, Camberwell,
Victoria 3124, Australia (a division of Pearson Australia Group Pty Ltd)
Penguin Books India Pvt Ltd, 11 Community Centre, Panchsheel Park, New Delhi – 110 017, India
Penguin Group (NZ), cnr Airborne and Rosedale Roads, Albany,
Auckland 1310, New Zealand (a division of Pearson New Zealand Ltd)
Penguin Books (South Africa) (Pty) Ltd, 24 Sturdee Avenue,
Rosebank, Johannesburg 2196, South Africa

Penguin Books Ltd, Registered Offices:
80 Strand, London WC2R 0RL, England

First published in the United States of America by The Penguin Press,
a member of Penguin Group (USA) Inc. 2005
Published in Penguin Books 2006

9   10   8

Copyright © Marina Lewycka, 2005
All rights reserved

PUBLISHER'S NOTE
This is a work of fiction. Names, characters, places, and incidents either are the product
of the author's imagination or are used fictitiously, and any resemblance to actual persons,
living or dead, business establishments, events, or locales is entirely coincidental.

THE LIBRARY OF CONGRESS HAS CATALOGED THE HARDCOVER EDITION AS FOLLOWS:
Lewycka, Marina, 1946–
A short history of tractors in Ukrainian / Marina Lewycka.
p.   cm.
ISBN 1-59420-044-0 (hc.)
ISBN 0 14 30.3674 2 (pbk.)
1. Ukrainians—Great Britain—Fiction.   2. Children of immigrants—Fiction.
3. Older parents—Fiction.   4. Young women—Fiction.   5. Older men—Fiction.
6. Widowers—Fiction.   7. Sisters—Fiction.   I. Title.
PR6112.E895S47 2005
823'.92—dc22
2004056542

Printed in the United States of America
Designed by Stephanie Huntwork

The H. W. Wilson Company has not published a new edition of *Sears List of Subject Headings: Canadian Companion* (CC6) since its sixth edition was published in 2001 because its editor, Lynne Lighthall, does not think that there are enough new subject headings to justify the publication of a new edition.

Canadian Subject Headings (CSH), published by the Library and Archives of Canada, is a list of English-language subject headings compatible with *Library of Congress Subject Headings* (LCSH) used to access and express the subject content of documents on Canada and Canadian topics. It is no longer published in a paper format and has been superseded by *CSH on the Web*, a free, up-to-date access to more than 6,000 English-language subject authority records (http://www.collectionscanada.ca/csh/index-e.html). The records are

FIGURE 5.7

This example is an illustration of:
- fiction book for young readers
- other title information (in 2nd level cataloging)
- subsidiary responsibility (in 2nd level cataloging)
- all illustrations are colored (in 2nd level cataloging)
- history note (in 2nd level cataloging)
- personal name added entry with optional designation of function(in 2nd level cataloging); note that the bibliographical form of name taken from the LC CIP is different from that on the title page
- added entry generated from history note (in 2nd level cataloging)
- 2 ISBNs qualified
- Library of Congress CIP showing AC subject headings for young readers
- two levels of cataloging for a children's collection

1st level cataloging

DiCamillo, Kate.
  The tale of Despereaux. -- Candlewick Press, 2006.
  267 p.

  ISBN-10: 0-7636-2528-9 ((pbk.).
  ISBN-13: 978-0-7636-2528-0 (pbk.).

  1. Fairy tales. 2. Mice -- Fiction. I. Title.

2nd level cataloging

DiCamillo, Kate.
  The tale of Despereaux : being the story of a mouse, a princess, some soup, and a spool of thread / Kate DiCamillo ; illustrated by Timothy Basil Ering. -- Cambridge, Mass. : Candlewick Press, 2006.
  267 p. : col. ill. ; 19 cm.

  Newberry Medal winner.
  Summary: The adventures of Despereaux Tilling, a small mouse of unusual talents, the princess that he loves, the servant girl who longs to be a princess, and a devious rat determined to bring them all to ruin.
  ISBN-10: 0-7636-2528-9 (pbk.).
  ISBN-13: 978-0-7636-2528-0 (pbk.).

  1. Fairy tales. 2. Mice -- Fiction. I. Ering, Timothy B., ill.
II. Newbery Medal. III. Title.

Fig. 5.7—Continues

FIGURE 5.7 *(continued)*

(title page)

THE TALE OF

Despereaux

being the story of a

mouse, a princess,

some soup, and

a spool of thread

Kate DiCamillo

illustrated by Timothy Basil Ering

CANDLEWICK PRESS
CAMBRIDGE, MASSACHUSETTS

(information on verso)

For Luke, who asked for
the story of an unlikely hero

This is a work of fiction. Names, characters, places, and incidents are either
the product of the author's imagination or, if real, are used fictitiously.

Text copyright © 2003 by Kate DiCamillo
Illustrations copyright © 2003 by Timothy Basil Ering

All rights reserved. No part of this book may be reproduced, transmitted,
or stored in an information retrieval system in any form or by any means,
graphic, electronic, or mechanical, including photocopying, taping, and
recording, without prior written permission from the publisher.

First paperback edition 2006

The Library of Congress has cataloged the hardcover edition as follows:
DiCamillo, Kate.
The tale of Despereaux / Kate DiCamillo ; illustrated by Timothy Basil Ering. — 1st ed.
p. cm.
Summary: The adventures of Despereaux Tilling, a small mouse of unusual
talents, the princess that he loves, the servant girl who longs to be a
princess, and a devious rat determined to bring them all to ruin.
ISBN-10 0-7636-1722-9 (hardcover)
ISBN-13 978-0-7636-1722-6 (hardcover)
[1. Fairy tales. 2. Mice — Fiction] I. Ering, Timothy B., ill. II. Title.
PZ8.D525 Tal 2003
[Fic]—dc21   2002034760

ISBN-10 0-7636-2529-9 (paperback)
ISBN-13 978-0-7636-2529-0 (paperback)

2 4 6 8 10 9 7 5 3 1

Printed in the United States of America

This book was typeset in Garamond Ludlow.
The illustrations were done in pencil.

Candlewick Press
2067 Massachusetts Avenue
Cambridge, Massachusetts 02140

Teacher's guide available at www.candlewick.com

---

available in both the MARC 21 format and thesaurus display. (MARC formats will be discussed in Chapter 7.) There is a monthly list of new and revised headings and an alphabetical list of subdivisions. The database is updated monthly and provides a large number of references, scope notes, and instructions setting topics in their Canadian context. The list of subdivisions provides French-language equivalents, and the database provides a link to *Répertoire de vedettes-matière* for equivalent French-language headings. Subject authority records for *Canadian Subject Headings* are also available in the AMICUS database. Registered AMICUS users can download CSH authority records in the MARC 21 format from AMICUS. (Although users must register to obtain entry to the AMICUS database, its use is free of charge.)

Libraries with significant collections of Canadian materials should use the appropriate list of Canadian terms from CC6 or CSH because both Sears and LCSH have a U.S.

FIGURE 5.8

This example is an illustration of:
- nonfiction book for young readers
- three authors
- edition statement
- series statement
- all illustrations are colored
- contents note expanded from that in CIP
- personal name added entries with bibliographic form of name taken from CIP
- series added entry
- ISBN qualified
- Library of Congress CIP with Library of Congress subject headings and AC subject headings for young readers
- 2nd level cataloging records for an adult collection and for a children's collection

2nd level cataloging for an adult collection

Silverstein, Alvin.
  The skeletal system / Alvin, Virginia, and Robert Silverstein. -- 1st ed. -- New York : Twenty-First Century Books, 1994.
    96 p. : col. ill. ; 26 cm. -- (Human body systems)

  Includes glossary, timeline, and index.
  ISBN 0-8050-2837-4 (acid-free paper).

  1. Musculoskeletal system -- Juvenile literature. 2. Skeleton -- Juvenile literature. I. Silverstein, Virginia B. II. Silverstein, Robert A. III. Title. IV. Series.

2nd level cataloging for a children's collection

Silverstein, Alvin.
  The skeletal system / Alvin, Virginia, and Robert Silverstein. -- 1st ed. -- New York : Twenty-First Century Books, 1994.
    96 p. : col. ill. ; 26 cm. -- (Human body systems)

  Includes glossary, timeline, and index.
  ISBN 0-8050-2837-4 (acid-free paper).

  1 Skeleton. 2. Bones. I. Silverstein, Virginia B. II. Silverstein, Robert A. III. Title. IV. Series.

N.B. A Canadian library would have the following publication/distribution statement:

New York : Twenty-First Century Books ; Markham, Ont. : Fitzhenry & Whiteside, 1994.

Fig. 5.8—Continues

FIGURE 5.8 *(continued)*

(title page)

THE
SKELETAL
SYSTEM

Dr. Alvin, Virginia, and Robert Silverstein

TWENTY-FIRST CENTURY BOOKS
A Division of Henry Holt and Company
New York

(information on verso)

Twenty-First Century Books
A Division of Henry Holt and Company, Inc.
115 West 18th Street
New York, NY 10011

Henry Holt ® and colophon are trademarks of
Henry Holt and Company, Inc.
Publishers since 1866

Text Copyright © 1994 Dr. Alvin Silverstein, Virginia Silverstein, and Robert Silverstein
Endpaper illustrations Copyright © 1994 Greg Harris
Illustrations Copyright © 1994 Lloyd Birmingham
All rights reserved.
Published in Canada by Fitzhenry & Whiteside Ltd.
195 Allstate Parkway, Markham, Ontario L3R 4T8

Library of Congress Cataloging-in-Publication Data
Silverstein, Alvin.
Skeletal system / Alvin, Virginia, and Robert Silverstein.—1st ed.
p.   cm. — (Human body systems)
Includes index.
1. Musculoskeletal system—Juvenile literature. 2. Skeleton—Juvenile literature. [1. Skeleton.
2. Bones.] I. Silverstein, Virginia B. II. Silverstein, Robert A. III. Title. IV. Series.
QP301.S55 1994

612.7'5—dc20   94-21421
                                                    CIP
                                                    AC

ISBN 0-8050-2837-4
First Edition 1994

Printed in Mexico
All first editions are printed on acid-free paper ∞.
10 9 8 7 6 5 4 3 2 1

Drawings by Lloyd Birmingham

Photo Credits
cover: Howard Sochurek/The Stock Market
p. 8: Karl Maslowski/Photo Researchers, Inc.; p. 11: Tom McHugh/Steinhart Aquarium/Photo
Researchers, Inc.; p. 13: Tom McHugh/Photo Researchers, Inc.; p. 16(l): Mark Marten/National
Library of Medicine/Photo Researchers, Inc.; p. 16(r): Science Photo Library/Photo Researchers,
Inc.; p. 17: Mark Marten/National Library of Medicine/Photo Researchers, Inc.; pp. 18, 21, and
63: Biophoto Associates/Photo Researchers, Inc.; pp. 22 and 24: CRNI/Science Photo
Library/Photo Researchers, Inc.; p. 29: Jean-Yves Ruszniewski/Agence Vandystadt/Photo
Researchers, Inc.; p. 35: NASA/Science Source/Photo Researchers, Inc.; p. 36: A. Sieveking/Petit
Format/Photo Researchers, Inc.; p. 39: Will and Deni McIntyre/Photo Researchers, Inc.; p. 41(l):
Ken Eward/Science Source/Photo Researchers, Inc.; p. 41(r): Don Fawcett/E. Shelton/Science
Source/Photo Researchers, Inc.; p. 55: Dave Roberts/Science Photo Library/Photo Researchers,
Inc.; p. 62: M. Abbey/Photo Researchers, Inc.; p. 66: Alfred Pasieka/Science Photo
Library/Photo Researchers, Inc.; p. 67: Richard T. Nowitz/Photo Researchers, Inc.; p. 70: NASA;
p. 74: Dept. of Clinical Radiology, Salisbury District Hospital/Science Photo Library/Photo
Researchers, Inc.; p. 76: Sue Ford/Science Photo Library/Photo Researchers, Inc.; p. 80: Scott
Camazine/Science Source/Photo Researchers, Inc.; p. 82: Catherine Ursillo/Photo Researchers,
Inc.; p. 88: John Reader/Science Photo Library/Photo Researchers, Inc.

orientation not suited to Canadian catalogs or collections of Canadian material in foreign catalogs. Some examples of the difference in the treatment of Canadian subject matter are:

- Native Canadians, including First Nations people, Métis, and Inuit (the LCSH heading **Indians of North America -- Canada** should always be investigated).

- War of 1812. An important war to Canadians, neither Sears nor LSCH recognize that battles were fought on Canadian soil and regard it as a totally U.S. war. It should also be noted that a different Dewey classification number would be assigned in Canadian libraries (971.03) rather than the one in Sears that applies to U.S. history (973.5). Classification numbers will be discussed in the next chapter.

- Because the subject heading **French Canadians** found in Sears and LCSH implies a connection to France, this subject heading should be changed to **Canadians, French-speaking** (from CSH if using LCSH headings) or **French-speaking Canadians** (from CC6 if using Sears).

Cataloging Tools Mentioned in Chapter 5

ALA Filing Rules (Chicago: American Library Association, 1980).

AMICUS (http://www.collectionscanada.gc.ca/amicus/index-e.html).

Association for Library Collections & Technical Services, Subject Analysis Committee, *Guidelines on Subject Access to Individual Works of Fiction, Drama, Etc.* 2nd ed. (Chicago: American Library Association, 2000).

Canadian Subject Headings (http://www.collectionscanada.ca/csh/index-e.html).

Cataloger's Desktop is available by subscription from LC's Cataloging Distribution Service (http://desktop.loc.gov).

Classification Web (http://www.classificationweb.net).

Library of Congress, Subject Cataloging Division, *Free-Floating Subdivisions: An Alphabetical Index*, 20th ed. (Washington, DC: Cataloging Distribution Service, 2008).

Library of Congress, Cataloging Policy and Support Office, Library Services, *Library of Congress Subject Headings*, 31st ed. (Washington, DC: Cataloging Distribution Service, 2009).

Library of Congress, Subject Cataloging Division, *Subject Cataloging Manual: Subject Headings*, 5th ed., 2004 cumulation (Washington, DC: Library of Congress, 1996–2004), plus updates issued in 2005, 2006, and 2008.

Rather, John C. *Library of Congress Filing Rules* (Washington, DC: Library of Congress, 1980).

Sears List of Subject Headings, 19th ed., Joseph Miller, editor, Barbara A. Bristow, associate editor (New York: H. W. Wilson, 2007).

Sears List of Subject Headings: *Canadian Companion,* 6th ed., edited by Lynne Lighthall (New York: H. W. Wilson, 2001). Also available online at http://www.hwwilson.com/Databases/sears.htm.

Exercises

Exercise 5A: LCSH headings are found in the CIPs for the following figures in this book. Check all these headings in Sears. If the subject headings are the same, write "same" in the spaces provided below; if Sears differs from LCSH, explain the difference, for example, "subject headings #1 and 3 are the same; #2 should be.. . ." Use extra paper if needed. The answers are found in the Appendix.

Figure 2.1 on page 6 _____

_____

Figure 3.2 on page 18 _____

_____

Figure 3.5 on page 29 _____

_____

Exercise 3C on page 32 _____

_____

Figure 4.1 on page 38 _____

_____

Figure 4.2 on page 40 _____

_____

Figure 4.3 on page 42 _____

_____

Figure 4.4 on page 44 _____

_____

Figure 4.5 on page 47 _____

_____

Figure 4.6 on page 50 _____

_____

Figure 4.7 on page 52 _____

_____

Exercise 4B on page 59 _____

_____

Exercise 5B: Do a first level bibliographic description using Sears subject headings and a second level bibliographic record using Library of Congress subject headings for the book pictured below as Exercise 5B using the traditional bibliographic style.

This book is 25 cm. in height, has many illustrations that include portraits and maps, 232 pages of text, and xvi preliminary pages.

(title page)

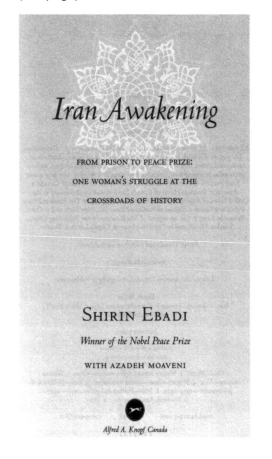

(information on verso)

PUBLISHED BY ALFRED A. KNOPF CANADA

Copyright © 2006 Shirin Ebadi

All rights reserved under International and Pan-American Copyright Conventions. No part of this book may be reproduced in any form or by any electronic or mechanical means, including information storage and retrieval systems, without permission in writing from the publisher, except by a reviewer, who may quote brief passages in a review. Published in 2006 by Alfred A. Knopf Canada, a division of Random House of Canada Limited, and simultaneously in the United States of America by Random House, an imprint of The Random House Publishing Group, a division of Random House, Inc., New York, and in Great Britain by Rider & Co., an imprint of The Random House Publishing Group, London. Distributed by Random House of Canada Limited, Toronto.

Knopf Canada and colophon are trademarks.

www.randomhouse.ca

Library and Archives Canada Cataloguing in Publication

Ebadi, Shirin
Iran awakening : a memoir of revolution and hope / Shirin Ebadi ; with Azadeh Moaveni.

Includes index.

ISBN-13: 978-0-676-97802-5
ISBN-10: 0-676-97802-9

1. Ebadi, Shirin. 2. Women human rights workers—Iran. 3. Women lawyers—Iran. 4. Women—Iran—Social conditions. 5. Iran—Politics and government—1979–1997. 6. Iran—Politics and government—1997– .
I. Moaveni, Azadeh, 1976– . II. Title.

DS318.84.E22A3 2006   323'.092   C2005-905736-X

4 6 8 9 7 5 3

Exercise 5C: Do a first level and a second level bibliographic record for the book pictured below as Exercise 5C using the traditional bibliographic style. There is no CIP.

This book is 20 cm. in height, has no illustrations, and has 261 pages of text.

Provide subject headings. This is a fiction book about Gertrude Stein and Alice B. Toklas. There is no difference between Sears and LCSH subject headings.

(information on verso)

(title page)

Monique Truong

THE BOOK OF SALT

𝒱

VINTAGE

Published by Vintage 2004

2 4 6 8 10 9 7 5 3

Copyright © Monique T. D. Truong, 2003

Monique Truong has asserted her right under the Copyright, Designs and Patents Act, 1988 to be identified as the author of this work

This book is sold subject to the condition that it shall not by way of trade or otherwise, be lent, resold, hired out, or otherwise circulated without the publisher's prior consent in any form of binding or cover other than that in which it is published and without a similar condition including this condition being imposed on the subsequent purchaser

First published in Great Britain in 2003 by
Chatto & Windus

Vintage
Random House, 20 Vauxhall Bridge Road,
London SW1V 2SA

Random House Australia (Pty) Limited
20 Alfred Street, Milsons Point, Sydney
New South Wales 2061, Australia

Random House New Zealand Limited
18 Poland Road, Glenfield,
Auckland 10, New Zealand

Random House (Pty) Limited
Endulini, 5A Jubilee Road, Parktown 2193,
South Africa

The Random House Group Limited Reg. No. 954009
www.randomhouse.co.uk/vintage

A CIP catalogue record for this book
is available from the British Library

ISBN 0 09 945545 5

Papers used by Random House are natural, recyclable products made from wood grown in sustainable forests. The manufacturing processes conform to the environmental regulations of the country of origin

Printed and bound in Denmark by
Nørhaven Paperback, Viborg

Exercise 5D: Do a first level bibliographic description using Sears subject headings and a second level bibliographic record using Library of Congress subject headings for the book pictured below as Exercise 5D using the traditional bibliographic style. There is no CIP.

This book is 12 cm. in height and 17 cm. in length, has illustrations, and has 47 pages of text.

(title page)

SCOTTISH COUNTRY RECIPES

compiled by
Johanna Mathie

illustrations by
H. J. Dobson RSW

Better wait on the cook
than on the doctor.
Scottish Proverb

SALMON

(information on verso)

Cover *front:* Hearth and Home *by Erskine Nicol*   *back:* Watermill near Pitlochry *by Birket Foster*
Title page: Granny's Blessing

Printed and Published by J. Salmon Ltd., Sevenoaks, England © Copyright

(information on back cover)

ISBN 1-902842-21-9

9 781902 842219

Exercise 5E: Do two second level bibliographic records for the book pictured below as Exercise 5E using the traditional bibliographic style: one for an adult collection using LCSH and one for a children's collection using AC headings.

This book is 22 cm. in height and 28 cm. in length, has illustrations, and has 186 pages of text. The book also includes an index.

(title page)

CLASSICAL KIDS

An Activity Guide to Life
in Ancient Greece and Rome

LAURIE CARLSON

CHICAGO
REVIEW
PRESS

(information on verso)

CIP:Library of Congress Cataloging-in-Publication Data

Carlson, Laurie M., 1952–
Classical kids : an activity guide to life in Ancient Greece and
Rome / Laurie Carlson.
        p.   cm.
Includes bibliographical references.
Summary: Demonstrates life in ancient Greece and Rome, and the
contributions of those cultures to modern civilization, through
hands-on activities such as making a star gazer, chiseling a clay
tablet, and weaving Roman sandals.
ISBN 1-55652-290-8
1. Greece–Social life and customs–Juvenile literature. 2. Rome–
Social life and customs–Juvenile literature. 3. Creative
activities and seat work–Juvenile literature. [1. Greece–
Civilization–To 146 B.C. 2. Rome–Civilization. 3. Handicraft.]
I. Title.
DE71.C26   1998
938–dc21
                                                           97-52676
                                                                CIP
                                                                 AC

Design and illustrations ©1998 by Fran Lee

©1998 by Laurie Carlson
All rights reserved
First edition
Published by Chicago Review Press, Incorporated
814 North Franklin Street
Chicago, Illinois 60610
ISBN 1-55652-290-8
Printed in the United States of America

Exercise 5F: Find the subject headings for the following topics in both Sears and LCSH. In some cases, there will be more than one subject heading needed. The first topic has been answered as an example:

Sport—mirror of American life
1. Sports — United States. 2. United States — Social life and customs (LCSH)

Same two subject headings (Sears)

Recipes for cooking with chocolate

Immigration : an issue for our times

_____

_____

Coping with business recessions

_____

_____

Museums in Vancouver, BC

_____

_____

Aids to geographical research (a list of books and periodicals)

_____

_____

Psychology applied to industry

_____

_____

The fight for women's suffrage in England

_____

_____

The ancient Japanese art of paper folding

_____

_____

Air conditioning and refrigeration

_____

_____

A pop-up book of farm animals in Montana

_____

_____

Recent exhibitions of postimpressionist art

_____

_____

Exercise 5G: You have a book about free trade between Canada and the United States. (Note that this book is <u>not</u> about NAFTA, an agreement that includes Mexico.) There are six possible subject headings that can be assigned to this book. (Think about ways in which catalog users might approach the information in this book.) List four or more subject headings.

_____

_____

_____

_____

Exercise 5H (for materials about Canada): Find the subject headings for the following topics in *Canadian Subject Headings*.
A book of pictures about the War of 1812 on Canadian soil

_____

Battle of Batoche in Saskatchewan

_____

The massacre of women students at the Ecole Polytechnique in Montreal

_____

_____

Additional Information

6

Classification

There are two aspects of subject analysis—subject headings and classification. Classification is the name applied to the arrangement of materials in a collection. In North American libraries, classification is used primarily to arrange materials on shelves according to their subjects, although some libraries apply classification numbers to remote-access electronic resources to help searchers find materials on the same subject. Classification is not used to arrange public catalogs, which are alphabetical. To rephrase this simply, books and other resources that are housed on shelves in the public areas of a library are arranged by call number (that is, classification number + shelf mark); bibliographic records in the library's catalog are arranged alphabetically by name, title, and subject heading access points.

The most popular classification systems in North America are the Dewey decimal classification (DDC) and the Library of Congress classification (LCC). DDC is found mainly in school library media centers and public libraries of all sizes, while LCC is used mainly in college and university libraries. This is not a hard and fast rule and there are many exceptions (for example, the University of Toronto Faculty of Information's library uses DDC and the Boston Public Library uses LCC). Translations of DDC into languages other than English now exceed thirty, and DDC is used to organize the national bibliographies of more than sixty countries.

DDC and LCC: A Comparison

Publication: Currently in its twenty-second edition, DDC is published in four printed volumes. A one-volume abridged fourteenth edition is also published for use with collections of up to 20,000 volumes. New issues of the printed editions are on a seven-year publication schedule. Both are available online with corrections and updates in *WebDewey* and *Abridged WebDewey*, which are mounted quarterly. Appropriate Library of Congress subject headings are suggested for the DDC numbers in the online editions.

LCC is published in forty-two volumes. New editions of each of the volumes appear separately at irregular intervals. LCC can also be found in an online version at *Classification Web*.

Structure: DDC and LCC both consist of schedules of numbers representing all topics in all disciplines in the universe of knowledge. DDC divides knowledge into ten main classes, LCC into twenty-one, deriving more main classes by separating some fields of study that DDC treats as part of a broader discipline. For example, DDC has one main class (the 300s) that includes sociology, political science, economics, law, and education. LCC has four main classes covering those same fields of study: H covers both sociology and economics; J covers political science; K covers law; and L covers education.

DDC employs more number-building than LCC through the use of auxiliary tables and repetitions of specific patterns of subdivision and sub-subdivision for numerous subjects, but its numbers do not match LCC's level of specificity although, theoretically, it could.

A second visible difference between the classifications is their notation. DDC's notation consists only of arabic numerals; LCC's is alphanumeric, using both capital letters and Arabic numerals. LCC's notation tends to be more flexible and economical than DDC's, since the number of characters it can combine and permute is larger (thirty-six for LCC versus ten for DDC). As a result, LCC numbers for the same topics can be much shorter.

A third and more significant difference between the two classifications is their structural approach. DDC is hierarchical and, for the most part, short numbers express broader topics, while long numbers represent narrower ones. The decimal point in DDC means the number sequence puts narrow topics after the broader ones to which they relate. For example, see the hierarchy for 793.734 on page 93 where the narrowest topic has the most numbers.

LCC, on the other hand, is a practical arrangement of LC's collection. It is not hierarchical, although some of its number spans do exhibit hierarchy. LCC often subdivides topics by alphabetizing their geographical or topical aspects. It also requires the publication of items on new topics before it establishes numbers for them, while DDC is more flexible. If it is clear that new topics have emerged, DDC numbers for them may be developed independently of the publication of specific items.

DDC provides mnemonics (memory aids) that operate throughout its schedules. For example, Table 1 allows the use of -03" for the dictionaries, encyclopedias, or concordances of a subject, and "-05" for serial publications devoted to a particular subject field. One learns that adding "-952" from Table 2 at the end of a DDC number probably means "Japan" and "-92" means biography. Schedules for LCC main classes are developed independently of one another, and LCC has no universal mnemonics. LCC's main classes have few, if any, internal mnemonics that apply throughout a class.

DDC has a single relative index that lists topics and numbers for the entire classification, while LCC indexes are specific only to individual volumes. Similarly, DDC has six auxiliary tables that apply to the entire classification, while LCC has myriad tables in every volume, but few of them apply to more than one span of numbers. Numbers from DDC tables are linked to numbers from the schedules (called "base" numbers) to subdivide them. Numbers from LCC tables may either be added arithmetically or linked to base numbers, depending, generally, on whether the table number is a digit (for example, 3 or 3.5) or a cutter number (that is, C3 or C3.5).

Co-extensive numbers: DDC and LCC practices dictate choosing a classification number, called a "co-extensive" number, that exactly matches the subject covered by an item. For example, an item titled *An Encyclopedia of Plants* is assigned a number for plants. Should the content of an item cover more than one subject, such as an item titled *An Encyclopedia of Animals and Plants*, it still is assigned only one number. To decide what the number should be, classifiers are expected to examine how much of the item is devoted to each subject. If one subject occupies more space in the book, the classification number for that subject is assigned. (If *An Encyclopedia of Animals and Plants* has 100 pages about plants and 200 about animals, it receives a number for animals.) If two or three subjects are covered equally, the LCC classification number assigned reflects the subject presented first in the work, but the DDC classification number reflects the number that comes first in the classification schedule; therefore, the appropriate DDC number for the example is the number for plants. If more than three subjects are covered, a broader number is assigned that includes all the individual subjects.

Librarians assume all copies of a title are assigned the same classification number. If a library has two copies of *An Encyclopedia of Animals and Plants*, it should not assign the number for animals to one and the number for plants to the second.

Literary warrant: This principle dictates that class numbers are created only after materials exist that require them. LCC creates classification numbers due to literary warrant, that is, a classification number is developed when LC receives materials for which a new classification is needed.

DDC is a universal classification and theoretically should not use literary warrant. However, no classification can anticipate or list all topics, and DDC is no exception. When new subjects appear, numbers for them are established, sometimes causing disruptions in the part of the classification where they occur. "Computers" is a good example of a topic that was established when the need for it emerged.

Assistance in understanding: A manual of more than 176 pages is provided in DDC's volume 4. In the fourteenth abridged DDC, the manual is found on 105 pages at the beginning of the book.

LC provides *Subject Cataloging Manual: Classification* in a separate loose-leaf publication of 378 pages, which is intended to help classifiers apply LCC according to LC policies.

Updates: DDC and LCC are updated on a continuous basis. The latest decisions on new, revised, and deleted classification numbers are disseminated online on their Web sites as well as via new printed publications. Both of the printed versions of DDC and abridged DDC provide a list of numbers from the previous edition than have been relocated in the present edition.

The Dewey Decimal Classification

Several principles underlie the organization and structure of DDC:

(1) *Decimal division.* Decimal division or division by tens is the primary method of dividing subjects used by DDC. It is a familiar and useful method of dividing things.

(2) *Classification by discipline.* The primary attribute applied in dividing knowledge is discipline, represented by the ten main classes.

(3) *Hierarchy.* The classification numbers in DDC move from broad categories to narrower ones and from these to still narrower ones until the narrowest possible category is reached.

(4) *Mnemonics.* Specific groups of numbers can represent the same topic in multiple places throughout the classification. A familiar example is the number "9," which stands for Geography and History in many instances: 900 = all Geography and History; 759 = Painting limited to a specific location. Adding 9 to the number for Manufacturing 670 = 670.9 makes it specific to a particular geographic location. Another example of mnemonics is found in the numbers for geographic locations: 41 = British Isles, when added to 670.9 stands for British manufacturing (670.941).

DDC is divided, first of all, into ten main classes, 100 divisions, and 1,000 sections. Main classes consist of spans of 100 whole numbers from XX0 to X99, where "X" stands for any digit between zero and nine.

The ten main classes are as follows:

Computer science, information, general works	(000–099)
Philosophy, parapsychology and occultism, psychology	(100–199)
Religion	(200–299)
Social sciences	(300–399)
Language	(400–499)
Natural sciences and mathematics	(500–599)
Technology (applied sciences)	(600–699)
The arts, fine and decorative arts	(700–799)
Literature (belles lettres) and rhetoric	(800–899)
History, geography, and auxiliary disciplines	(900–999)

Each class is divided into ten divisions; for example, the divisions in Technology are:

General topics, e.g., dictionaries, organizations, etc.	(600–609)
Medicine and health	(610–619)
Engineering and allied operations	(620–629)
Agriculture and related technologies	(630–639)
Home and family management	(640–649)
Management and auxiliary services	(650–659)
Chemical engineering and related technologies	(660–669)
Manufacturing	(670–679)
Manufacture of products for specific uses	(680–689)
Buildings	(690–699)

These divisions are, in turn, divided into ten sections; for example, the ten sections in medical sciences are:

General topics	(610)
Human anatomy, cytology, histology	(611)
Human physiology	(612)
Personal health and safety	(613)
Forensic medicine; incidence of injuries, wounds, disease; public preventative medicine	(614)
Pharmacology and therapeutics	(615)
Diseases	(616)
Miscellaneous branches of medicine; surgery	(617)
Other branches of medicine; gynecology	(618)
(Experimental medicine relocated in DDC22 to 616.027)	(619)

These sections include one whole number and all the decimally extended classification numbers falling between it and the next whole number; for example, 618.1 is devoted to gynecology, while 618.2 covers obstetrics. Some sections are subdivided extensively, while others have few subdivisions and extend only one, two, or three digits beyond the decimal point. For example, 618.24 covers prenatal care and preparation for childbirth, and 618.244 covers exercise for pregnant women.

Catalogers will find lists of divisions and sections in the first few pages of volume 2 of the unabridged printed edition and on pages 177–188 of the abridged printed edition under the heading "Summaries." Small summaries are found at the start of each new main class and sometimes at the beginning of a subclass or still-smaller spans of numbers.

The hierarchy of a Dewey classification number is highlighted in the following example. The DDC in the CIP for a book titled *Everything Scrabble* is 793.734. This reads as:

7	=	The arts, fine and decorative arts
79	=	Recreational and performing arts
793	=	Indoor games and amusements
793.7	=	Games not characterized by action
793.73	=	Puzzles and puzzle games
793.734	=	Word games, including Scrabble

The Tables

DDC provides six auxiliary tables of numbers to be linked to numbers from the main schedules to further subdivide them. Numbers from the tables can never be used alone, but are to be added to numbers from the schedules. Students and beginning catalogers are likely to use only Tables 1 and 2. The application of Tables 3 to 6 can be learned later when a cataloger has more experience in assigning classification numbers.

Table 1, Standard Subdivisions, is used often to narrow the meaning of numbers from the main schedules and may be used with any number from the main schedules provided there is no instruction *not* to do so. The basic pattern of Table 1 numbers is:

-01	=	Philosophy and theory of a subject
-02	=	Miscellany
-03	=	Dictionaries, encyclopedias, concordances
-04	=	Special topics (only used when specifically directed in the schedules)
-05	=	Serial publications
-06	=	Organizations and management
-07	=	Education, research, related topics
-08	=	History and description with respect to kinds of persons
-09	=	Historical, geographic, persons (i.e., biographical) treatment

When -09 is added to a number to limit a subject to a particular location, the standard procedure is to specify the place by linking a number for it from Table 2, the list of numbers for geographic areas, historical periods, and persons. An explicit instruction is given at the start of 093-099 to add numbers that further specify location from Table 2. Sometimes, instructions in the main schedules dictate dropping the zero. Sometimes, the instructions dictate more than one zero, for example, a book about farm horses in the United States would be 636.100973.

The instructions at the beginning of 913–919 (geography of and travel in . . .) tell the classifier to add the numbers from Table 2 to the base 91. Therefore, while the history of the United States is 973, the geography of and the travel in the United States is 917.3; the history of Ontario is 971.3 and its geography and travel is 917.13.

Biography

DDC states that the preferred method of classifying a biography is to place it with the topic with which the person is closely connected. The CIP for the biography of Ayaan Hirsi Ali in Figure 6.1 has classified the book in the history of the Netherlands in the period since 1980 (949.2073) with the subdivision 092 for biography added to it. However, many libraries prefer to have their biographies shelved together, and there are several options in common use to do this. DDC suggests using one of the following for collections of biographies:

- Use the 920-928 schedule, for example, 923.1 (heads of state).

- Use 920.71 for biographies of men and 920.72 for biographies of women.

In addition, one of the following practices are used in many libraries:

- Use 920 for collected biographies and 921 for individual biographies.

- Use 92 for individual biographies.

- Use B (indicating biography) for individual biographies.

DDC's Relative Index

One of Dewey's original ideas in the decimal classification was the Relative Index, which, in the twenty-second printed edition, occupies 229 pages in volume 4 and 216 pages in the fourteenth printed abridged edition. This alphabetic listing of topics and associated classification numbers is a valuable tool for classifiers.

Dewey intended the index to be used as a final check *after* a number was assigned. A number should not be assigned from the index without consulting the schedules. A particular subject term often turns out to be associated with more than one number, and often the meaning of a term in colloquial language differs from its meaning in the DDC. The most important classification decision is the main class to which an item belongs, not what number represents its subject. Once the main class is determined, a classifier should move down its hierarchy to locate the appropriate classification number, going from main class to division, from division to section, and then looking further within a section to the proper expression of the desired subject.

CIP Records and DDC Classification

Most CIP records provide a DDC number after the tracing, and in the Library of Congress' CIPs the DDC numbers are followed by another number indicating the edition of the DDC schedules from which the number was derived. In Figure 6.1, "B 22" follows the Dewey number. The "B" stands for biography, alerting the cataloger to the possibility of

FIGURE 6.1

This example is an illustration of:
- 2 ISBNs
- abridged and unabridged Dewey classification numbers
- Sears and Library of Congress subject headings the same
- Library of Congress CIP
- two levels of cataloging

1st level cataloging

Hirsi Ali, Ayaan.
  Infidel. -- Free Press, c2007.
  xii, 353 p.

  ISBN-13: 978-0-7432-8968-0.
  ISBN-10: 0-7432-8968-4.

  1. Politicians -- Netherlands -- Biography. 2. Muslims --
Netherlands -- Biography. 3. Refugees -- Netherlands -- Biography.
I. Title.

2nd level cataloging

Hirsi Ali, Ayaan.
  Infidel / Ayaan Hirsi Ali. -- New York : Free Press, c2007.
  xii, 353 p. ; 23 cm.

  ISBN-13: 978-0-7432-8968-0.
  ISBN-10: 0-7432-8968-4.

  1. Politicians -- Netherlands -- Biography. 2. Muslims --
Netherlands -- Biography. 3. Refugees -- Netherlands -- Biography.
I. Title.

Recommended DDC: 949.2073092
Recommended abridged DDC: 949.207092

The publication/distribution area in a Canadian catalog would read:

New York ; Toronto : Free Press, c2007.

Fig. 6.1—Continues

FIGURE 6.1 *(continued)*

(title page)

(information on verso)

INFIDEL

Ayaan Hirsi Ali

FREE PRESS

New York London Toronto Sydney

FREE PRESS
A Division of Simon & Schuster, Inc.
1230 Avenue of the Americas
New York, NY 10020

For reasons of privacy, certain names in this book have been changed.

FREE PRESS and colophon are trademarks of Simon & Schuster, Inc.

For information about special discounts for bulk purchases,
please contact Simon & Schuster Special Sales at
1-800-456-6798 or business@simonandschuster.com

DESIGNED BY ERICH HOBBING

Manufactured in the United States of America

17 19 20 18

Library of Congress Cataloging-in-Publication Data
Hirsi Ali, Ayaan.
Infidel / Ayaan Hirsi Ali.
p. cm.
1. Politicians—Netherlands—Biography. 2. Muslims—Netherlands—Biography.
3. Refugees—Netherlands—Biography. I. Title.

DJ292.H57 A3 2007
949.207'3092 B 22   2006049762

ISBN-13: 978-0-7432-8968-9
ISBN-10: 0-7432-8968-4

using a local biography scheme, and the "22" indicates that the classification number was taken from DDC's twenty-second edition (DDC22), the edition in use at this writing. If there is some other number following the classification number, the DDC must be checked in DDC22 to affirm that the number is still valid, because in each DDC edition, some numbers have been revised, expanded, or deleted. A senior cataloger can alert the beginning cataloger about major revisions that have taken place since the last edition and about the parts of the DDC that are unlikely to have changed, thus cutting down on the numbers to be checked. For example, in the CIP for Figure 4.1 on page 38, the Dewey number 595.77'2 is followed by "dc21," which indicates that the number was taken from DDC's twenty-first edition. This means that 595.772 must be looked up in DDC22 (or 595.77 in Abridged DDC14) to see whether the number has changed.

Some CIPs do not indicate the DDC edition from which the classification number was derived. In this case, the cataloger determines the validity of the DDC by looking at the date the book was published. DDC22 was published in 2003; therefore, the DDCs assigned to books cataloged from 2004 onward do not need to be checked in DDC22 (or in Abridged DDC14). Books published previous to that date must be checked (some books published in 2003 were cataloged before DDC22 appeared).

Figure 2.3 on page 8 has two CIPs from different cataloging agencies with different DDCs. LC has 616.8'092 for a biography of someone associated with diseases of the nervous system, while NLC (that is, Library and Archives of Canada) has 540.92 for a biography of someone associated with chemistry. A cataloger must do some research to determine that the author is a well-known neurologist and that the correct DDC is 616.8'092. This is a good example of an instance where CIP catalogers were given limited information about the content of a book and relied on the word "chemistry" (hence, the 540.92 classification) in the title to determine subject content.

Abridged And Unabridged DDC

Many small libraries use the abridged DDC due to its less detailed DDC numbers and a cheaper purchase price. Therefore, in these libraries the DDC provided in CIP records might need to be changed to the less detailed numbers found in the abridged DDC. (Many numbers in the abridged DDC are the same as the corresponding number in the unabridged edition.) The method most frequently used in CIPs to show where numbers have been expanded is an apostrophe, called a *prime mark* or *hash mark*, which is placed at the end of the basic number and again after each complete expansion. By knowing where the expansions begin and end, a library can opt to copy what is most appropriate to its needs. One library might use the entire number with all its expansions; a second library might want only the basic number, excluding the expansions; and a third might prefer something in between, such as accepting the first expansion but nothing more. For example, the DDC in Figure 6.1 has only one prime mark (949.207'3092). The numbers before the prime mark (949.207) are the numbers for the history of the Netherlands from 1901, while the unabridged DDC has divided the history even farther, with 949.2073 standing for the history of the Netherlands since 1980. Biography is indicated by "092," which can be added to either the abridged or the unabridged DDC if desired. However, a small library may have very few materials on the history of the Netherlands and could use only the basic number for Netherlands history, 949.2, even though no prime mark in the CIP indicates this.

Prime marks in CIPs are sometimes indicated by a slash, and the slash is always used in MARC records emanating from national cataloging agencies (see Chapter 10). An example of this can be found in Figure 2.1 on page 6. Here, the DDC is written as 001.9/6 (the "22" following indicates that this number was taken from the twenty-second edition of DDC). 001.9 stands for controversial knowledge, and this number is further subdivided to 001.96 for errors, delusions, and superstitions.

It should be noted that prime marks do not indicate the only ways that long DDC numbers can be shortened. This can be determined only by consulting the schedules. The expansions are meaningful expressions of subject matter and should not be cut off in the middle, causing a loss of meaning. For example, the DDC number for the topic "Models of helicopters" is 629.1331352—a very long number. A small library having a policy of using a maximum of five numbers would cut off the number after the first "3," leaving an item about helicopter models in 629.13. Doing that, however, destroys the meaning of the basic topic, "Aircraft models," represented by the slightly longer number 629.1331, and puts the material in the much broader subject of "Aeronautics." Assigning 629.13 would mix together materials about real planes and helicopters with materials about model aircraft, which seems less desirable than separating them, even in a library or media center with a small collection.

Completing the DDC Call Number

Classification is only part of a call number. Most libraries add shelf marks to the DDC classification number for an effective arrangement of books on shelves in public areas that serve local needs. Small collections may not bother to add many shelf marks because it is not difficult to distinguish small numbers of titles with the same classification number. Large collections tend to add more because they need to distinguish large numbers of similar titles on the same subject. There are two kinds of shelf marks added to DDC classification numbers.

Call Letters: Call letters are taken from the first one, two, or three letters of the primary entry. Small public libraries and school library media centers might be able to shelve materials successfully using only a simple call letter in addition to the classification number. Larger collections will need two or three letters to distinguish books in their collections on the same subject. Looking once again at the classification number in Figure 6.1 on page 96, the call number for this book in small library might be 949.2 H; in a library with a bigger collection of materials relating to Netherlands history, the call number might be 949.2092 HI or 949.207092 HIR, depending on the size of the collection.

Cutter Numbers: Charles Cutter initiated the practice of creating brief alphanumeric symbols consisting of an initial letter followed by one or more digits representing subsequent letters to substitute for full names or other words. The result is to alphabetize them using fewer characters than if they were spelled out in full. The symbols are known as cutter numbers, and the practice of assigning them is called "cuttering." There are two-number and three-number tables that are used to assign these cutter numbers and that are easily learned. For example, the cutter number for Figure 6.1 taken from the *Cutter-Sanborn Three-Figure Author Table* is H617. The only deviation from this policy is for biography, where the cutter number or call letters of the biographee is listed before that of the author. For example, the call letters for a biography of Charles Dickens by John Brown would be DIC BRO and the three-figure call number D555 B814.

Title Letters: In order to distinguish among the works of prolific authors, letters from significant words in individual titles may be added in order to form unique call numbers that alphabetize the person's works on the shelf. Title letters usually are lowercased and added to the end of the call letters or numbers. The number of letters to be added is a matter of local policy, but it is wise to add enough to avoid potential conflicts, even though it may not be practical to add a great many. Choosing the appropriate title letters to use as shelf marks may require extra thought if classifiers are faced with many items by the same author with titles such as "The Mystery of the . . . " or "The Lonely Planet Guide to. . . ."

Unique Call Numbers: Each item in a library collection does not have to be given a unique call number. Libraries that want each title (not item) in their collection to have a unique call number are likely to assign shelf marks that distinguish individual titles, such as adding title letters described above. In some libraries where copy numbers are added, each item bears a unique call number, such as "copy 1," "copy 2," etc. (Some people think the bar code has replaced copy numbers, but that is wrong. Each bar code is a unique number and identifies the particular copy to which it is given. To some degree, bar codes echo the much earlier practice of assigning an accession number to each item added to a library's collection.)

Department Locations: If two copies of an item are purchased, for example, one for a main library collection and one for a branch, the main library and/or branch designations are likely to appear first, followed by the same call number. Or, if one copy is purchased for the reference collection and a second for the circulating collection, the designations identifying them will precede the rest of the call number. Reference departments, for example, might be identified as "R" or "Ref."

Library of Congress Classification

The description of the Library of Congress classification (LCC) in this book is less detailed than that given to DDC because library technician students, beginning catalogers, and distance-education students are unlikely to have access to the forty-two volumes that contain LCC. Because of this, there will be no exercises for LCC at the end of this chapter.

LCC was designed at the turn of the twentieth century specifically to shelve the Library of Congress's own collection efficiently, without regard to whether the classification might be adopted by other libraries. Subject experts in various disciplines were asked to create numbers for LC's then-current holdings and leave space for those parts of the disciplines in which future expansion could be anticipated. As a result, LCC volumes do not follow a single method of dividing and subdividing subjects, though they do share some characteristics, as described below.

Unlike DDC, LCC is not a hierarchical classification, although it does exhibit some elements of hierarchy. Because of this, the most important disadvantage of LCC for patrons of public libraries and school library media centers is the loss of browsability that results from using a nonhierarchical system like LCC.

Unlike Sears and LC subject headings, where the skills learned in using one system can be easily transferred to the other, the skills learned in either DDC or LCC are not so easily transferable. As mentioned, each schedule is an individual entity in which the division and organization of the subjects need not relate to that of any other schedule. Therefore, individual schedules may be in their first, second, third, or later editions. Since the late twentieth century, new editions are identified solely by the publication year (for example, at this writing, the R schedule, which covers medicine, is in its 2008 edition, and the PN schedule, which covers general literature, is in its 2007 edition).

LCC's Principles

Several principles underlie the organization and structure of LCC:

1. *Literary warrant.* This principle, which dictates that classes or numbers be established only when materials exist that require them, is fundamental to LCC. LCC was not designed primarily to organize knowledge as DDC does, but solely to organize LC's collection. Because of this, LCC did not need to provide numbers for topics outside of LC's collecting interests. However, those collecting interests are so numerous, broad, and varied, and LC collects so much more material than other libraries do, that general library classifiers can expect to find all the numbers they need in LCC.

2. *Classification by discipline.* Like DDC, LCC divides knowledge first into disciplines. In all, twenty-one single-letter main classes represent the disciplines in LCC, in contrast to only ten in DDC.

3. *Close classification.* A high level of detail and precision in classification is known as "close classification." LCC's close classification was designed to enable scholars to make fine distinctions between documents on similar topics.

4. *Alphabetical arrangement.* One of LCC's basic tools in dividing topical areas is the use of alphabetical arrangements. These arrangements are notated by means of

FIGURE 6.2 Library of Congress Classification in Forty-Two Volumes

A	General Works (2008)
B-BJ	Philosophy, Psychology (2008)
BL-BQ	Religion (General), Hinduism, Judaism, Islam, Buddhism (2008)
BR-BX	Christianity, Bible (2008)
C	Auxiliary Sciences of History (2008)
D-DR	History (General) and History of Europe (2007)
DS-DX	History of Asia, Africa, Australia, New Zealand, etc. (2008)
E-F	History: America (2007)
G	Geography, Maps, Anthropology, Recreation (2007)
G tables	Geographic Cutter Numbers; Tables G1548-G9804 (pdf format, no charge)
H	Social Sciences (2008)
J	Political Science (2008)
K	Law (General) (2005)
K tables	Form division tables for Law (2005) (apply to all K subclasses except KD, KE, & KF)
KB	Religious law (2004)
KD	Law of the United Kingdom and Ireland (2008)
KDZ, KG-KH	Law of the Americas, Latin America, and the West Indies (2008)
KE	Law of Canada (2008)
KF	Law of the United States (2008)
KJ-KKZ	Law of Europe (2008)
KJV-KJW	Law of France (2008)
KK-KKC	Law of Germany (2008)
KL-KWX	Law of Asia, Eurasia, Africa, Pacific Area, and Antarctica (2008)
KZ	Law of nations (2007)
L	Education (2008)
M	Music and Books on Music (2007)
N	Fine Arts (2007)
P-PZ tables	Language and Literature Tables (2006)
P-PA	Philology and Linguistics (General), Greek Language and Literature, Latin languages and literature (2005)
PB-PH	Modern European languages (2005)
PJ-PK	Oriental Philology and Literature, Indo-Iranian Philology and literature (2008)
PL-PM	Languages of Eastern Asia, Africa, Oceania, Hyperborean, Indian, and Artificial Languages (2006)

Fig. 6.2—Continues

FIGURE 6.2 *(continued)*

PN	Literature (General) (2007)
PQ	French, Italian, Spanish, and Portuguese literatures (2008)
PR, PS, PZ	English and American Literature, Juvenile Belles Lettres (2008)
PT	German, Dutch, and Scandinavian literature (2009)
Q	Science (2009)
R	Medicine (2008)
S	Agriculture (2008)
T	Technology (2007)
U-V	Military Science, Naval Science (2008)
Z	Bibliography, Library Science, Information Resources (2006)

cutter numbers, that is, translations of verbal terms into brief, alphanumeric terms consisting of the initial letter followed by one or more numbers representing the subsequent letters of the words. Some LCC cutter numbers are mnemonics for words, but some cutter numbers are not linked to words at all and merely represent a particular kind of topical division.

5. *Geographical arrangement.* Geographical subarrangements are also heavily favored in LCC, sometimes in addition to and sometimes in place of alphabetical arrangements. This is logical for a system used by legislative researchers seeking information specific to various jurisdictions. When the geographical locations are expressed by means of cutter numbers, the subarrangement is also alphabetical. When locations are expressed in numeric terms or through the use of other devices, alphabetization does not play a role.

6. *Economy of notation.* LCC uses mixed notation, employing both alphabetic and numeric characters. This gives it far greater flexibility to represent a large number of classes with fewer characters. Although it is not always the case, LCC frequently requires fewer characters to represent topics at very narrow levels of hierarchy than are required by DDC. For example, a book by Joseph R. Matthews titled *The Evaluation and Measurement of Library Services* was assigned a six-character LCC number (Z678.85) and an eight-character DDC number (025.10973).

7. *Relative location.* Similar to DDC, LCC employs the principle of relative location, although its use of geographic and alphabetic subarrangements tends to fragment materials related to one another in a topical hierarchy.

The Format of LCC Numbers

An LCC call number consists of a classification number to which are added one or more shelf marks, just as a DDC number does. The classification elements all have the following two parts:

• One, two, or, occasionally, three capital letters identifying the subject discipline (main class, first letter) and a broad subdivision within it (subclass, second and third letters).

For example, K stands for law; KF stands for law of the United States; and KFG stands for the law of the state of Georgia. Most disciplines have a maximum of two capital letters, but the G (geography) and K (law) schedules have numbers that contain three.

- A sequential whole number from 1 to 9999, sometimes, extended decimally, representing narrower subdivisions of the topic, as can be seen in the Matthews book cited in the previous section.

Some LCC classification numbers also may include the following:

- A cutter number that is part of the classification, not a shelf mark, representing a further subarrangement by a topic, a geographic location, a language, a form or genre, a time period, etc. For example, a book by Maria Giulia Amadasi Guzzo and Eugenia Equini Schneider titled *Petra* was assigned the classification number DS154.9.P48, to which the shelf marks A45 2002 were added. The first cutter number stands for the location. (Note: The first cutter number in an LCC call number is preceded by a period. When the call number includes more than one cutter number, only the first is preceded by a period. The reason for this punctuation protocol has been lost.)

- A second cutter number, also part of the classification number, not a shelf mark, representing a specific kind of material.

- A date (for example, the dates of financial crises are part of class numbers for materials on those events).

Tables: Tables used in LCC apply to a single schedule or, in many instances, to a single number or limited span of numbers. Tables in LCC take several forms. Some provide an array of whole numbers and/or whole numbers with decimal extensions that are added arithmetically to a base number to create more narrowly defined subarrangements of topics. Other tables consist of cutter numbers intended to follow a number from the schedules, subdividing it further by topic or geographic location. A different type consists of special "A" and "Z" cutter numbers that do not represent characters in words but define categories or forms.

Completing the LCC Call Number

The assignment of shelf marks for materials classified using LCC is not the same as those assigned to DCC. In Figure 6.1 on page 96, the CIP gives the complete LCC with appropriate shelf marks, while the DDC is given without shelf marks. This is because the items that LC catalogs are part of its collection and, therefore, have a place on LC's shelves for which a cutter number is established, whereas the DDC is not used by LC to house its collection. In a LC CIP, the DDC number is added solely as an aid to catalogers.

Once the LCC classification number is assigned, a series of shelf marks are added to it that provide an exact address for the item on local library shelves. The first shelf mark is usually a cutter number representing the main entry of the work, although at times it may represent a different element, such as subject or geographic location. The cutter number is followed by one or more added marks, including publication dates, title marks, collection locations (these often precede the classification number, as in the call number of a reference department copy of a book that begins with an "R," followed by a classification number and all the other shelf marks), copy numbers, and/or other elements mandated by local policies.

Libraries that assign LCC numbers need not use the same shelf marks assigned by LC. For example, in LCC call numbers, the shelf mark "I58" stands for the name "Intner." Very small libraries may substitute letters alone, calling them cutter letters instead of cutter numbers, for example, and Intner's book could be cuttered "I," "In," or "Int."

Only LC can establish official cutter numbers, but any cataloger can create local cutters at any time for use in their libraries. Later, if a cataloger discovers that LC has cataloged the same item using a different cutter number, he or she can choose to change the local number to conform to LC or continue to use the locally assigned number. Beginning catalogers should follow the library's policy in this matter.

Cutter numbers are usually followed by dates. The dates used as shelf mark elements are publication dates. The publication years, given in Arabic numerals, are added to LCC call numbers after the cutter numbers regardless of how editions are expressed in the items themselves, that is, whether they are numbered editions (2nd, 3rd, etc.), named editions (revised, enlarged, etc.), or editions actually identified by years of publication (2007 edition).

The Canadian Connection

With DDC:

Canadian literature: Many Canadian libraries wish to distinguish Canadian literary works from other English-language literary works. DDC provides the option of adding an uppercase "C" as a prefix to 810 (for English-language works) and to 840 (for French-language works). It is the policy of the Library and Archives of Canada (LAC) to extend this option to distinguish Canadian literature in all languages throughout the literature schedules.

With LCC:

Canadian law: LC has one Canadian-related schedule, KE for Canadian law developed in association with the National Library of Canada (the name later changed to LAC). However, most Canadian law libraries and many corporate libraries use a modified KF classification developed by the York University Law Library.

Canadian history and *Canadian literature*: LC does not use the two schedules developed by LAC for materials relating to Canadian history (*Class FC: A Classification for Canadian History*) and Canadian literature (*Class PS8000: A Classification for Canadian Literature*), both of which are available on the LAC Web site. These LAC schedules supply more specific classification numbers for Canadian content than the main LCC schedules.

Cataloging Tools Mentioned in Chapter 6

Abridged Dewey Decimal Classification and Relative Index. 14th ed. (Dublin, OH: OCLC, 2003).

Abridged WebDewey (http//:www.oclc.org/us/en/dewey/versions/abridgedwebdewey/default.htm).

Charles Ammi Cutter, *Two-Figure Author Table* (Chicopee Falls, MA: H. R. Hunting; distr. Westport, CT: Libraries Unlimited, 1969–); *Cutter-Sanborn Three-Figure Author Table*, Swanson-Swift revision (Westport, CT: Libraries Unlimited, 1969); cutter tables are also available at http://www.cuttertables.com.

Class FC: A Classification for Canadian History, 2nd ed. (Ottawa: Library and Archives of Canada, 1994), plus four *Additions and Changes* to 2006 (http://collectionscanada.ca/9/11/index-e.htm).

Class PS8000: A Classification for Canadian Literature, 3rd ed. (Ottawa: Library and Archives of Canada, 2003) (http://collections canada.ca/9/15/index-e.html).

Classification Web (http://www.loc.gov/cds/classweb).

Dewey Decimal Classification and Relative Index. 22nd ed. 4 vols. (Dublin, OH: OCLC, 2003).

Knight, Tim, ed. *KF Classification Modified for Use in Canadian Law Libraries.* Rev. (North York, ON: York University Law Library, 1994; distributed by Canadian Association of Law Libraries).

Library of Congress Classification. 30th ed. (Washington, DC: Library of Congress, 2007).

Subject Cataloging Manual: Classification (Washington, DC: Library of Congress Cataloging Distribution Service, 2008).

WebDewey (http://www.oclc.org/dewey).

Exercises

The answers to these exercises are found in the Appendix.

Exercise 6A: Look at the CIPs in the versos of the figures and exercises in Chapter 2 to 6.

1. Why do some of the classification numbers need to be checked?

2. List the figures or exercises in Chapters 2 to 6 that have Dewey classification numbers, which should be checked in the most recent edition of DDC.

3. Which ones need to be changed? If so, how would you change them?

Exercise 6B: When would you use Table 1 and when would you use Table 2?

Exercise 6C: Explain the meaning of each digit for the DDC classification number 686.232705. (See page 93 for an example of how this is done.) After you have completed this, state the meaning of the number.

Exercise 6D: To what subject do both **599.665** and **636.1** apply? Briefly describe the content of the book for which you would use each of them.

Exercise 6E: The classification numbers **915.67** and **956.7** both apply to Iraq. Explain the meaning of the difference.

Exercise 6F: A book about foreign relations between the United States and Canada. Start the number with 327 and add appropriately to this number as directed in DDC:

1. if the book were housed in a U.S. library.

2. if the book were housed in a Canadian library.

Exercise 6G: Provide Dewey decimal classification numbers for the following topics:

(a)	field hockey	_____
(b)	divorce mediation	_____
(c)	descriptive cataloging	_____
(d)	understanding acute leukemia	_____
(e)	winter Olympic games	_____

(f)   Royal Canadian Mounted Police   _____

(g)   space walks   _____

(h)   insurance against earthquakes   _____

(i)   Hinduism   _____

(j)   a journal of physics   _____

(k)   life expectancy in China   _____

(l)   museums in Cleveland   _____

(m)   a history of the education of women   _____

(n)   picture book of church buildings   _____

(o)   Great Barrier Reef, Australia   _____

(p)   collection of humorous riddles   _____

(q)   legendary heroes   _____

(r)   medical dictionary of substance abuse   _____

(s)   distance education in Winnipeg   _____

(t)   design of fire escapes   _____

Exercise 6H: For the book pictured as Exercise 6H below:

(a) Make a bibliographical record at the first level of cataloging that includes Sears subject headings and an abridged DDC number.

(b) Make a bibliographical record at the second level of cataloging that includes Library of Congress subject headings and an unabridged DDC number.

This book has 64 pages of plates, 374 pages of text, and 13 unnumbered pages at the beginning of the book. It is 23 cm. in height.

(title page)

M Y T H S   A N D   L E G E N D S
S E R I E S

THE BRITISH

M. I. EBBUTT

WITH ILLUSTRATIONS
FROM DRAWINGS AND
FAMOUS PAINTINGS

(information on verso)

Previously published by George G Harrap & Co

This edition published 1986 by Bracken Books
a division of Bestseller Publications Ltd
Brent House, 24 Friern Park, North Finchley
London

Copyright © BRACKEN BOOKS 1985

All rights reserved. No part of this publication
may be reproduced, stored in a retrieval system,
or transmitted, in any form or by any means, electronic,
mechanical, photocopying, recording or otherwise,
without the prior permission of the copyright holder.

ISBN 0 946495 83 1

Printed and bound in Great Britain
by Clark Constable, Edinburgh and London

BRACKEN BOOKS
LONDON

If your library has a card catalog, skip Chapter 7 and read Chapter 8, "Copy Cataloging," next.

Additional Information

Additional Information

7

Computer Coding

Introduction

In this book we started learning to catalog by working with CIP records found on the verso of many books. Most of these CIP records use the traditional catalog card format, and this book's instructions continued to use this format as a starting point because the format was familiar to new catalogers. However, automation has changed the card catalog into an online public access catalog (OPAC), eliminating the necessity of fitting bibliographic information onto a catalog card. It is now acceptable to add as many subject headings and notes as needed to cover an item's content. Automation also allows the bibliographic records in today's OPACs to be presented in the ways that the library's administration deems most useful to its users.

Putting call numbers, main and added entries, bibliographic descriptions, subject headings, and other details into computers requires that the data be presented in a way that a computer can accept the data and identify the parts, and programs can be written instructing the processor to manipulate the data. This is called computer coding (also known as computer mark-up), and the sets of instructions used to do it are called encoding protocols or mark-up languages. Figure 7.1 demonstrates a type of bibliographic record seen in many of today's catalogs in which encoding protocols have been overlaid on the data but do not become an integral part of the contents. In this example of overlaying protocols on data, the parts of a bibliographic description have been identified by adding explanatory prefixes. The data from the CIP in Figure 4.1 on page 38 are displayed in a different way in Figure 7.1 than they are in the bibliographic record in Figure 4.1. This is not the only way that OPACs display a bibliographic record. There are many other ways in which bibliographic information can be presented in an automated catalog. Beginning catalogers should visit several local libraries—academic, public, school, and special—or access their online catalogs to see the different ways in which their OPACs display bibliographic information.

Careful examination of the display in Figure 7.1 reveals that two things have changed in the encoded version. First, as one would expect from the explanatory phrases used in the protocol, the AACR2 names of the descriptive elements have been added to identify the kind of data each part presents. Second, some of the ISBD punctuation mandated by AACR2, principally, the full stop-space-dash-space required to divide one descriptive element from another, has been dropped.

The MARC (MAchine-Readable Cataloging) format is the primary encoding or mark-up language for library data, but other protocols or mark-up languages are beginning to be used as well. Five MARC formats have been developed, beginning with the one for bibliographic data. The others are for authority data, holdings data, classification data, and community information. This chapter will discuss the MARC bibliographic format.

FIGURE 7.1   Demonstration of Possible OPAC Display

```
Author:               Spielman, A. (Andrew).
Main title:           Mosquito : a natural history of our most
                      persistent and deadly foe / by Andrew Spielman
                      and Michael D'Antonio.
Edition:              1st ed.
Published/created:    New York : Hyperion, c2001.
Description:          xix, 247 p., [8] p. of plates : ill. (some
                      col.), maps. ; 22 cm.
Notes:                Includes index.
ISBN:                 ISBN 0-7868-6781-7.
Subjects:             Mosquitoes.
                      Mosquitoes as carriers of disease.
Additional author     D'Antonio, Michael.
Call number:          595.722 Sp54
```

MARC 21 is the current standard for the United States and Canada. However, each major bibliographic network has developed its own version of MARC, changing some of the displays and some of the protocols for its own users. Thus, the initial fields (called fixed fields) can appear in different forms on the screen depending on which database is searched. Some fields that are not part of the official standard were established by individual networks for use by their participants only, and individual computer systems reproduce certain codes differently. Therefore, fixed fields other than those listed in Figure 7.3 will not be discussed in this book because beginning catalogers will have to learn to use the version of these fixed fields in the libraries in which they will work.

Elements of MARC Records

A MARC record is not a new type of cataloging. It is an encoded version of a catalog record prepared using the current standards accepted by North American libraries. It contains all the information included in a catalog record plus added information needed for computer processing. The cataloging data (main and added entries, title statements, edition statements, etc.) are the content of the record; everything else added to the content to identify individual records and their parts is the coding. Figure 7.2 shows a MARC record for the OPAC record in Figure 7.1 in which the coding is highlighted (highlighting is used here as a demonstration). The parts that are not highlighted comprise the record content.

MARC records are divided into parts called *fields* (for example, in Figure 7.2 there are eleven fields from 020 to 700), which are then divided into smaller parts called *subfields* (for example, field 300 has three subfields). Fields have names known as *tags* (for example, field 700 is known as the personal name added entry tag). Subfields have names known as *subfield codes* (for example, $b is the subfield code for the publisher in field 260). Fields also contain field-specific computer instructions called *indicators* (for example, the indicator "1" after field 245 tells the computer to make a title added entry, and indicator "0" tells the computer that there are no words to be to be ignored at the beginning of the title

FIGURE 7.2   MARC Encoding Highlighted in Bold Type

```
020       $a 0-7868-6781-7.
082 00 $a 595.722 $b Sp54 $2 22
100  1    $a Spielman, A. $q(Andrew).
245 10 $a Mosquito : $b a natural history of our most persistent and
             deadly foe / $c by Andrew Spielman and Michael D'Antonio.
250       $a 1st ed.
260       $a New York : $b Hyperion, $c c2001.
300       $a xix, 247 p., [8] p. of plates: $b ill. (some col.), maps ; $c
             22 cm.
504       $a Includes index.
650   0 $a Mosquitoes.
650   0 $a Mosquitoes as carriers of disease.
700  1    $a D'Antonio, Michael.
```

when this title added entry becomes part of the alphabetical file of titles. Such nonfiling words are definite and indefinite articles, such as "a," "an," "the," and their foreign equivalents. All the names and symbols used by the format to code the record content—everything other than the content itself—are called *content designators.*

Content Designation

The process of encoding or marking up a catalog record in MARC format has several names. It is likely to be called plain "coding," not "encoding," which is seldom heard. Library catalogers rarely use the term "marking-up" for MARC coding, perhaps because the term and the idea of mark-up languages originated among computer specialists, not librarians. Because MARC fields are known by tags, the process is often called "tagging" or both "coding and tagging." The most formal name for the process is "content designation," so called because the MARC protocols name (or "designate") elements of cataloging data (or "content") in the record. Thus, MARC protocols designate content, and the process by which it is done is called content designation.

Fields

As stated above, coded catalog records are divided first into fields. Each element of the catalog record has a corresponding field, identified by a specific tag, into which the content for that element is put. Tags are always three-digit numbers. Once catalogers using MARC format learn the tags for the elements, they soon refer to elements by their tags. For example, a cataloger might ask, "Does this book have a 250?" meaning "Does this book have an edition statement?" When a computer programmed to accept catalog records in MARC format encounters the three consecutive digits 250 at the beginning of a field, it interprets the information that follows (up to the mark indicating the end of the field) as an edition statement.

The 8XX series of tags is used for complicated series statements and for holdings data. The 9XX series of tags is reserved for local use. There are many more tags that will be used by experienced catalogers for more complex materials.

FIGURE 7.3 MARC Field Tags Most Likely Used by Beginning Catalogers in Cataloging Books

010	Library of Congress control number (see Chapter 8)
020	International Standard Book Number (ISBN)
050	Library of Congress call number
082	Dewey decimal classification number
090	Sometimes used for local call number
100	Personal name main entry
110	Corporate name main entry
111	Meeting name main entry
240	Uniform title
245	Transcribed title and statement of responsibility
246	Varying form of title
250	Edition statement
260	Publication/distribution information
300	Physical description
440	Transcribed series statement that will be given an added entry
490	Series statement given no added entry or given an added entry in a form that differs from the series statement appearing in the descriptive cataloging
500	General notes
504	Bibliography note
505	Formatted contents note
520	Summary
600	Personal name subject added entry
610	Corporate name subject added entry
611	Meeting name subject added entry
650	Topical term subject added entry
651	Geographic name subject added entry
700	Personal name added entry
710	Corporate name added entry
711	Meeting name added entry

Subfields

Fields are further subdivided into subfields. Each subfield has a name consisting of a delimiter symbol that identifies it as a subfield and a subfield code identifying which kind of subfield it is. Delimiters, which precede all subfield codes, may display differently in different computer systems, but are usually represented either by the double cross symbol ($\neq$) or the dollar sign ($) or other symbols ($ is arbitrarily used in this chapter).

Subfields are field-specific, for example, in 300, *subfield $a* is the extent of an item; in 260, *subfield $a* is the place of publication. Note in Figure 7.2 that field 245 has been divided into three subfields: 245 *subfield $a* is the title proper, *subfield $b* contains other title information, and *subfield $c* is the statement of responsibility.

Subfield codes are either single letters or numbers. For example, in field 082 (Dewey decimal call number field), $a contains the classification number, $b the shelf mark, and $2 the number of the DDC edition used. In Figure 7.2, the subfield code $2 22 indicates that this DDC number was taken from the twenty-second edition of DDC. The CIP for this book (see page 38) shows that the DDC in the CIP was taken from DDC21. The subfield code $2 22 in Figure 7.2 indicates that this DDC has been checked and is a valid number in DDC22.

Indicators

Two character positions are available between the tag and the subfield codes for field-specific instructions called *indicators*, which tell a computer how to manipulate the data content of the field. Indicators are not defined for every field, but those that are defined are always specific to the field in which they appear. Fields can have no indicators, one indicator that can appear in either the first or the second position, or two indicators. For example, field 300 has none; field 100 has one indicator in the first position, which "indicates" that the main entry personal name is a forename, a surname, or a family name. Field 650 has one indicator in the second position, which indicates the thesaurus from which the subject heading was taken (0 for LCSH, 1 for LC's AC headings, etc.); and field 245 has two indicators—the first directs the computer either to make or not make a title added entry and the second indicator directs the computer on how many nonfiling characters to ignore if making a title added entry. Indicators enable programmers to write programs for computers to display or suppress selected pieces of data as well as to index and file the data correctly and perform other database management tasks properly.

Figure 7.4 demonstrates a MARC record for a book entered under a title with an abridged DDC number not assigned by LC and a Sears subject heading. (The traditional-style record for this book is found as Figure 4.3 on page 41.)

Figure 7.5 demonstrates the MARC coding for a children's collection in the traditional-style record in Figure 5.8 on page 78 with abridged DDC chosen by LC. Note that

FIGURE 7.4   MARC for Figure 4.3

```
020      $a 0262072459 (hc. : alk. paper).
082 14 $a 302.23 $b N469 $2 14
245 00 $a New media, 1740-1915 / $c edited by Lisa Gitelman and
            Geoffrey B. Pingree.
260      $a Cambridge, Mass. : $b Pingree, $c c2003.
300      $a xxxiii, 271 p. ; $c 23 cm.
440    0 $a Media in transition
504      $a Includes index.
650    7 $a Mass media $x History. $2 Sears 19
700    1 $a Gitelman, Lisa.
700    1 $a Pingree, Geoffrey B.
```

FIGURE 7.5   MARC for Figure 5.8

```
020      $a 0805028374 (acid-free paper).
082 04   $a 612.7 $b SIL $2 14
100 1    $a Silverstein, Alvin.
245 14   $a The skeletal system / $c Alvin, Virginia, and Robert
           Silverstein.
250      $a 1st ed.
260      $a New York : $b Twenty-First Century Books, $c 1994.
300      $a 96 p. : $b col. ill. ; $c 26 cm.
440   0  $a Human body systems
504      $a Includes glossary, timeline, and index.
650   1  $a Skeleton.
650   1  $a Bones.
700 10   $a Silverstein, Virginia B.
700 10   $a Silverstein, Robert A.
```

when a catalog record contains AC headings, they are found in the usual MARC format subject fields (650, 651, etc.) with the second indicator coded "1" instead of "0."

Cataloging Tools Mentioned in Chapter 7

MARC 21 Format for Bibliographic Data (http://www.loc.gov/marc/bibliographic).

Exercises

Prepare a second level bibliographic description MARC record for the each of the figures indicated below using fields 020, 082, and 100–799. Use the *MARC 21 Format for Bibliographic Data* (http://www.loc.gov/marc/bibliographic/) to complete these exercises. Assign Dewey decimal classification numbers from the unabridged edition and LCSH for all exercises unless directions are given to assign abridged Dewey decimal classification numbers and Sears subject headings. Use either cutter numbers or call letters to complete the call numbers.

The first five books have CIP records; the next five books do not. Answers to these exercises will be found in the Appendix.

Exercise 7A

(title page)   **(information on verso)**

MARCH

A NOVEL

—m—

Geraldine Brooks

PENGUIN BOOKS

PENGUIN BOOKS
Published by the Penguin Group
Penguin Group (USA) Inc., 375 Hudson Street, New York, New York 10014, U.S.A.
Penguin Group (Canada), 90 Eglinton Avenue East, Suite 700, Toronto,
Ontario, Canada M4P 2Y3 (a division of Pearson Penguin Canada Inc.)
Penguin Books Ltd, 80 Strand, London WC2R 0RL, England
Penguin Ireland, 25 St Stephen's Green, Dublin 2, Ireland (a division of Penguin Books Ltd)
Penguin Group (Australia), 250 Camberwell Road, Camberwell,
Victoria 3124, Australia (a division of Pearson Australia Group Pty Ltd)
Penguin Books India Pvt Ltd, 11 Community Centre,
Panchsheel Park, New Delhi – 110 017, India
Penguin Group (NZ), cnr Airborne and Rosedale Roads, Albany,
Auckland 1310, New Zealand (a division of Pearson New Zealand Ltd)
Penguin Books (South Africa) (Pty) Ltd, 24 Sturdee Avenue,
Rosebank, Johannesburg 2196, South Africa

Penguin Books Ltd, Registered Offices:
80 Strand, London WC2R 0RL, England

First published in the United States of America by Viking Penguin,
a member of Penguin Group (USA) Inc. 2005
Published in Penguin Books 2006

7   9   10   8   6

THE LIBRARY OF CONGRESS HAS CATALOGED THE HARDCOVER EDITION AS FOLLOWS:
Brooks, Geraldine.
March / Geraldine Brooks.
p.   cm.
ISBN 0-670-03335-9 (hc.)
ISBN 0 14 30.3666 1 (pbk.)
1. United States–History–Civil War, 1861–1865–Fiction.   2. March family (Fictitious
characters)–Fiction.   3. Fathers and daughters–Fiction.   4. Soldiers–Fiction.   I. Title.
PR9619.3B7153M37 2004
823'.914–dc22   2004049496

Printed in the United States of America
Set in Caslon Book   Designed by Francesca Belanger

This book has 280 pages of text followed by pages numbered 1–3 containing "A Reader's Guide to March" and pages number 1–9 containing "A Conversation With Geraldine Brooks." It is 20 cm. in height.

Exercise 7B

(title page)

g a b r i e l   g a r c í a   m á r q u e z

one
hundred
years
of
solitude

Translated from the Spanish by Gregory Rabassa

P E R E N N I A L 📖 C L A S S I C S

(information on verso)

Assistance for the translation of this volume was given by the Center for Inter-American Relations.

This book was originally published in Argentina in 1967 by Editorial Sudamer-icanos, S.A., Buenos Aires under the title *Cien Años de Soledad*.

A hardcover edition of this book was published in 1970 by Harper & Row, Publishers.

ONE HUNDRED YEARS OF SOLITUDE. English translation copyright © 1970 by Harper & Row, Publishers, Inc. All rights reserved. Printed in the United States of America. No part of this book may be used or reproduced in any manner whatsoever without written permission except in the case of brief quotations embodied in critical articles and reviews. For information, address HarperCollins Publishers, Inc., 10 East 53rd Street, New York, NY 10022.

HarperCollins books may be purchased for educational, business, or sales pro-motional use. For information please write: Special Markets Department, HarperCollins Publishers, Inc., 10 East 53rd Street, New York, NY 10022.

First HarperPerennial edition published 1992.

First Perennial Classics edition published 1998.

Perennial Classics are published by HarperPerennial, a division of HarperCollins Publishers.

Designed by Nyamekye Waliyaya

Library of Congress Cataloging-in-Publication Data
García Márquez, Gabriel, 1928–
   [Cien años de soledad. English]
   One hundred years of solitude / Gabriel García Márquez. 1st Perennial Classics ed.
     p. cm.
   ISBN 0-06-074045-0
   1. Macondo (Imaginary place)—Fiction.   2. Latin America—Social conditions—Fiction.   3. Epic literature.   I. Title
PQ8180.17.A73C513 1998
863—dc21   98–24308

03 04 05 06 ❖/RRD 10 9 8 7 6 5 4 3 2 1

This book is 21 cm. in height and has 458 pages of text.

Exercise 7C

(title page)

PEOPLE OF
THE ICE WHALE

Eskimos, White Men, and the Whale

David Boeri

A Harvest/HBJ Book
Harcourt Brace Jovanovich, Publishers
San Diego   New York   London

(information on verso)

I have changed the names of several Gambell whaling captains
and a woman in Barrow. Benjamin, Isaac, Solomon,
and Sarah are all pseudonyms.

The illustrations on pages 83, 120, 124, and 125, the first illustration
on page 165, and the illustrations on pages 177 and 216 are from
The Marine Mammals of the Northwestern Coast of North America,
by Charles W. Scammon (originally published in 1874; reprinted by
Dover Publikations, Inc., New York, 1968). The second illustration on
page 165 is from *Sea Guide to Whales of the World* by Lyall Watson,
illustrated by Tom Ritchie (New York: E. P. Dutton, 1981).
The drawing of the bowhead whale on pages 5 and 103 and
the three maps on page xvi, 13, and 238 are by Judy Lyons.

Library of Congress Cataloging in Publication Data
Boeri, David.
People of the ice whale.
Reprint. Originally published: New York: E.P. Dutton, © 1983.
"A Harvest/HBJ book."
1. Eskimos—Alaska—Fishing.   2. Indians of North
America—Alaska—Fishing.   3. Whaling—Alaska.   4. Bowhead
whale.   5. Wildlife conservation—Alaska. I. Title.
E99.E7B677   1985   305.8'97'07987   84-45840
ISBN 0-15-671660-7

Designed by Nancy Etheredge
Printed in the United States of America.
First Harvest/HBJ edition
A B C D E F G H I J

This book is 20 cm. in height and has 285 pages of text with illustrations, maps, and xvi preliminary pages. It has bibliographical references.

The Dewey decimal classification number in the CIP record is difficult for beginning catalogers to check because Table 5 must be used. Go to DDC's volume 3, page 1009, that suggests alternate numbers for North American native peoples. Provide a DDC number based on these options.

Exercise 7D

(title page)

Ken McGoogan

F A T A L   P A S S A G E

(information on verse)

The Untold Story of John Rae,
the Arctic Adventurer Who Discovered the Fate of Franklin

Fatal Passage: The Untold Story of John Rae,
the Arctic Adventurer Who Discovered the Fate of Franklin
Copyright © 2001 by Kenneth McGoogan.
 For information address
HarperCollins Publishers Ltd,
55 Avenue Road, Suite 2900,
Toronto, Ontario, Canada M5R 3L2

www.harpercanada.com

HarperCollins books may be purchased for educa-
tional, business, or sales promotional use.
For information please write:
Special Markets Department,
HarperCollins Canada,
55 Avenue Road, Suite 2900,
Toronto, Ontario, Canada M5R 3L2

First PerennialCanada edition

The financial assistance of the Alberta Foundation for the Arts
is gratefully acknowledged.

Canadian Cataloguing in Publication Data

McGoogan, Kenneth, 1947–
Fatal passage : the untold story of John Rae, the Arctic
adventurer who discovered the fate of Franklin

"A Phyllis Bruce book"
Includes bibliographical references and index.
ISBN 0-00-638659-8

1. Rae, John, 1813–1893.
2. Arctic regions – Discovery and exploration –
    British.
3. Northwest, Canadian – Discovery and exploration –
    British.
4. Franklin, John, Sir, 1786–1847.
5. Northwest Passage – Discovery and exploration –
    British.
6. Explorers – Scotland – Biography.
I. Title

FC3961.1.R33M33 2001   917.1904'Y'092   C2001-902529-7
G635.R25M33 2001

RRD 9 8 7 6 5 4 3

Printed and bound in the United States
Set in Monotype Janson

A Phyllis Bruce Book
Harper*Perennial*Canada
HarperCollins*PublishersLtd*

───────────

This book is 24 cm. in height and has 327 pages of text with illustrations, portraits, and one map.

Exercise 7E

(title page)

The

GHOST MAP

The Story of London's Most Terrifying Epidemic—

and How It Changed Science, Cities,

and the Modern World

STEVEN JOHNSON

RIVERHEAD BOOKS

a member of Penguin Group (USA) Inc.

New York   2006

(information on verso)

RIVERHEAD BOOKS
Published by the Penguin Group
Penguin Group (USA) Inc., 375 Hudson Street, New York, New York 10014, USA · Penguin
Group (Canada), 90 Eglinton Avenue East, Suite 700, Toronto, Ontario M4P 2Y3, Canada
(a division of Pearson Penguin Canada Inc.) · Penguin Books Ltd, 80 Strand, London
WC2R 0RL, England · Penguin Ireland, 25 St Stephen's Green, Dublin 2, Ireland (a division
of Penguin Books Ltd) · Penguin Group (Australia), 250 Camberwell Road, Camberwell, Victoria
3124, Australia (a division of Pearson Australia Group Pty Ltd) · Penguin Books India Pvt Ltd,
11 Community Centre, Panchsheel Park, New Delhi–110 017, India · Penguin Group (NZ),
Cnr Airborne and Rosedale Roads, Albany, Auckland 1310, New Zealand (a division of
Pearson New Zealand Ltd) · Penguin Books (South Africa) (Pty) Ltd, 24 Sturdee Avenue,
Rosebank, Johannesburg 2196, South Africa

Penguin Books Ltd, Registered Offices:
80 Strand, London WC2R 0RL, England

Copyright © 2006 by Steven Johnson
All rights reserved. No part of this book may be reproduced, scanned,
or distributed in any printed or electronic form without permission. Please do
not participate in or encourage piracy of copyrighted materials in violation
of the author's rights. Purchase only authorized editions.
Published simultaneously in Canada

The passage from Walter Benjamin's "Theses on the Philosophy of History"
is from *Illuminations*, translated by Harry Zohn.
A list of illustration credits can be found on page 300.

Library of Congress Cataloging-in-Publication Data

Johnson, Steven, date.
Ghost map : the story of London's most terrifying epidemic—and how it changed science,
cities, and the modern world / Steven Johnson.
p.   cm.
Includes bibliographical references and index.
ISBN 1-59448-925-4
1. Cholera—England—London—History—19th century.   I. Title.
RC133.G6J64   2006   2006023114
614.5'14—dc22

Printed in the United States of America
3   5   7   9   10   8   6   4

BOOK DESIGN AND MAP ON PAGES XII AND XIII BY MEIGHAN CAVANAUGH

While the author has made every effort to provide accurate telephone numbers and
Internet addresses at the time of publication, neither the publisher nor the author assumes
any responsibility for errors, or for changes that occur after publication. Further, the
publisher does not have any control over and does not assume any responsibility
for author or third-party websites or their content.

This book is 20 cm. in height and has 299 pages of text and illustrations that include portraits and maps.

Assign an abridged Dewey decimal classification number and Sears subject headings.

Exercise 7F

(title page)

Plain Tales from the Raj

*Images of British India
in the Twentieth Century*

CHARLES ALLEN

Edited in association with Michael Mason
Introduction by Philip Mason

(information on verso)

An *Abacus* Book

First published in Great Britain in 1975
by André Deutsch Limited
First published in paperback in 1976 by Futura
This edition published in 2000 by Abacus

A CIP catalogue record for this book
is available from the British Library.

ISBN: 0 349 10497 2

Printed and bound in Great Britain
by Clays Ltd, St Ives plc

Abacus
A Division of
Little, Brown & Company (UK)
Brettenham House
Lancaster Place
London WC2E 7EN

This book is 24 cm. in height and has 287 pages of text and 8 pages of plates with illustrations that include facsimiles. There is a "Preface to New Edition" on pages 9–12.

Exercise 7G

(title page)

(information on verso)

Rick Steves'

German

Phrase Book & Dictionary

Fifth Edition

**AVALON
TRAVEL**

Avalon Travel Publishing, 1400 65th Street, Suite 250, Emeryville, CA 94608, USA

Avalon Travel Publishing is a division of Avalon Publishing Group, Inc.

Printed in the United States of America by Worzalla.
Fifth edition. First printing May 2003.

ISBN 1-56691-519-8

Europe Through the Back Door Managing Editor:
  Risa Laib
Europe Through the Back Door Editor:
  Cameron Hewitt
Avalon Travel Publishing Editor: Matt Orendorff
Translation: Julia Klimek, Martin Minich
Phonetics: Risa Laib, Cameron Hewitt
Production & Typesetting: Matt Orendorff
Cover Design: Kari Gim
Maps & Graphics: David C. Hoerlein, Zoey Platt
Photography: Rick Steves, Dominic Bonuccelli,
  Andrea Johnson
Front cover photos:
  foreground– © Anderson Ross/Getty Images/
Photodisc/2003; background– © Royalty-Free/CORBIS

Distributed to the book trade by
Publishers Group West, Berkeley, California

Although the author and publisher have made every effort to provide accurate, up-to-date information, they accept no responsibility for loss, injury, bad bratwurst, or inconvenience sustained by any person using this book.

———

This book is 15 cm. in height and has 279 pages of text, xi preliminary pages, and illustrations that include maps.

Exercise 7H

(title page)

Tea

Addiction, Exploitation and Empire

ROY MOXHAM

(information on verso)

Carroll & Graf Publishers
An imprint of Avalon Publishing Group, Inc.
161 William Street
New York
NY 10038-2607
www.carrollandgraf.com

First Carroll & Graf edition 2003

First published in the UK by Constable
an imprint of Constable & Robinson Ltd 2003

ISBN 0-7867-1227-9

Printed and bound in the EU

CARROLL & GRAF PUBLISHERS
New York

———

This book is 22 cm. in height and has 271 pages of text, xii preliminary pages, and illustrations that include maps. It has a bibliography and an index.

The content of this book deals with British activities in the tea trade.

Exercise 7I

(title page)

(information on colophon)

LONELY PLANET OFFICES

Australia
Head Office
Locked Bag 1, Footscray, Victoria 3011
☎ 03 8379 8000, fax 03 8379 8111
talk2us@lonelyplanet.com.au

USA
150 Linden St, Oakland, CA 94607
☎ 510 893 8555, toll free 800 275 8555
fax 510 893 8572
info@lonelyplanet.com

UK
72–82 Rosebery Ave,
Clerkenwell, London EC1R 4RW
☎ 020 7841 9000, fax 020 7841 9001
go@lonelyplanet.co.uk

Hungary

Steve Fallon
Neal Bedford

Published by Lonely Planet Publications Pty Ltd
ABN 36 005 607 983

© Lonely Planet Publications Pty Ltd 2006

© photographers as indicated 2006

Cover photographs: Swimmers at public baths in the Hungarian capital of Budapest, Adam Woolfitt/APL/Corbis (front); Traffic trails on the Széchenyi Chain Bridge, Jonathan Smith/Lonely Planet Images (back). Many of the images in this guide are available for licensing from Lonely Planet Images: www.lonelyplanetimages.com.

Printed through Colorcraft Ltd, Hong Kong.
Printed in China

(information on barcode)

ISBN 1 - 74104 - 223 - 2

USA $21.99
UK   £14.99

5TH EDITION

9 781741 042238

This book is 20 cm. in height and has 424 pages of text with colored illustrations that include maps. It has an index.

This is a guidebook for people planning to travel in Hungary.

Exercise 7J

(title page)

Library Daylight

Tracings of Modern Librarianship, 1874-1922

(information on verso)

Edited by Rory Litwin

Published by Library Juice Press, 2006

With an introduction by Dr. Suzanne Stauffer

Library Juice Press
PO Box 3320
Duluth, MN 55803

http://libraryjuicepress.com/

ISBN 13: 978-0-9778617-4-3
ISBN 10: 0-9778617-4-0

Printed on acid-free paper.

Library Juice Press, LLC
Duluth, Minnesota

———

This book is 23 cm. in height and has 248 pages of text with no illustrations. It has an index.

This is a collection of journal articles, newspaper clippings, meeting reports, etc., written by different people about librarianship in the United States, much of it relating to public libraries.

Additional Information

Additional Information

8

Copy Cataloging

Introduction

Copy cataloging is the name given to operations that use existing catalog records as data sources for materials being cataloged, editing the records in accordance with local policies so they can be incorporated into local catalogs. It is an appropriate name because the local catalogers are, essentially, *copying* relevant information from the source records they use instead of building entirely new records "from scratch" by transcribing information directly from the materials. Another name for copy cataloging is *derived cataloging*, because local library records are derived from preexisting source records. This chapter uses the name copy cataloging.

Copy cataloging has two principal goals: saving time and money. A third goal might be ensuring the quality of the records entered into the local library catalog, but achieving this depends on the likelihood that the source records are of better quality than the agency would achieve if they did "from scratch" original cataloging. Copying poor quality records cannot provide a good local catalog.

- *Saving time*: The idea behind copy cataloging is that, in order to produce a finished catalog record, local catalogers need not spend the time it takes to transcribe data carefully from materials to create bibliographic descriptions, determine descriptive and subject headings, perform authority control activities, classify the material, and enter all the data into the catalog. Instead, the process is as fast as 1-2-3: (1) find a source record to copy, (2) make certain it matches the material being cataloged, and (3) edit a few elements that vary locally, such as call numbers. *Voilà*! The work is done. Instead of taking as much as forty minutes to an hour for one book, copy cataloging might take ten minutes or less.

- *Saving money*: Because the largest proportion of cataloging cost is paying for catalogers' time, speeding up the cataloging process enables local libraries to save money as well as time, even though they usually pay for access to source records. On balance, the cost of access to source records is believed to be less than the cost of original cataloging for all materials a library acquires for its collections.

- *Ensuring quality*: As already mentioned, the quality of copy cataloging depends on the quality of its sources. Records that originate at the Library of Congress and the national libraries of Canada and the United Kingdom provide the highest quality data available. However, copying records that do not match the material being cataloged, or records that match but are created by people who do not observe cataloging standards or are careless about transcription and data entry, introduces errors into local catalogs that cause retrieval problems for the patrons who search them. Source quality is discussed further in the next section, "Policy Issues."

Policy Issues

In order to save the most time and money, library administrators may erroneously assume that source records can be accepted and used in local catalogs "as is," with no further work. Though ideal, this is rarely the case, because selected elements from outside local libraries do not apply to local situations. In particular, call numbers are likely to be different from those of the source libraries, but call numbers are not the only problems. Five policy areas usually have to be considered: acceptable sources, record fullness, errors in the source copy, call numbers, and tracings.

1. *Acceptable sources*: Copy catalogers recognize that all source records are not equally good. Sometimes source records lack needed data and sometimes they contain errors. Using them without adding missing data or correcting the errors debases the local catalog and makes it less effective for local patrons. Doing the work to upgrade poor quality source records takes time and costs the local library money. Thus, although network contracts usually require that existing records be used if they match the materials being cataloged, this provision is hard to enforce. Copy catalogers might not recognize matches due to errors or omissions. To ensure they avoid wasting time and work only with quality records, copy cataloging supervisors develop lists of unacceptable and preferred sources.

   Catalogers recognize a hierarchy of quality that rates national libraries at the top, providing the best quality records, followed by trained members of the Program for Cooperative Cataloging (PCC) known to meet current standards, large research libraries that maintain knowledgeable cataloging staffs, and, perhaps, a selection of other libraries known to do good cataloging. Most contributors recognize the importance of accurate data and do their best to enter quality original cataloging into the database.

2. *Record fullness*: Local policies concerning bibliographic levels govern the amount of information provided in original cataloging. AACR2 bibliographic level 1 omits several data elements that are important for libraries with large collections and libraries whose patrons depend on their catalogs for research. Even when level 2 is the norm, optional elements can be omitted on a routine basis. Some libraries opt for minimal level cataloging (such as OCLC K level or PCC core records) for some of the materials given original cataloging, especially if they face a combination of heavy workloads and shrinking resources. A longtime debate continues over the relative value of less-than-full cataloging versus no cataloging at all.

   Despite cataloging rules and network contract obligations, some libraries omit data they do not use, such as notes, standard numbers, added entries, and numerous subject headings. (One of the authors worked in a library that filed only title added entries, but no others. Among her tasks was crossing out the unwanted added entries from Library of Congress unit cards.) Some libraries assign no more than one or two subject headings to nonfiction materials. Some do not check authority files and establish new headings however they appear on materials without worrying about using only authorized name forms or potential conflicts.

3. *Errors*: Catalog records prepared and processed by human beings are bound to contain some errors, despite quality-control procedures and other efforts to keep network databases clean as a whistle. The policy issue is what to do about errors found in source copy. Should they be allowed to remain, or should they be corrected? Three choices are possible: correct all errors; correct no errors; or correct selected errors. The first choice is the most costly, and policy makers should be certain that having an error-free catalog is worth the expense. The second choice contributes most to loss of quality and presents the most problems for local patrons trying to search in the catalog. The third choice is a compromise solution that tries to balance cost and quality.

Catalogers generally divide errors into those that affect retrieval, such as misspelled titles, names, or subject headings, and those that do not, such as misspelled notes or incorrect punctuation. Knowing that it costs the library money to correct errors that do not affect retrieval and are unlikely to create misunderstandings, local libraries may choose not to correct them. In that event, rules must be devised that clearly identify the "must correct" errors for data-entry staff. Also, library staff must be prepared for patrons to see the uncorrected errors on their screens and, possibly, complain about them.

4. *Call numbers*: Of all the elements of a standard catalog entry, the call number is most likely to vary from the norm. A call number is a shelf address in a local library collection. There is little to be gained from making it conform to the shelf address of any other library, including that of the Library of Congress. Local classification and shelf-marking policies may mandate differences from recommendations of standard tools and the practices of leading libraries. Typical examples include the following:

- Not classifying fiction; instead, arranging it alphabetically by authors' surnames in a separate "Fiction" section; or, classifying fiction by genre into a number of sections such as "General Fiction," "Short Stories," "Westerns," "Science Fiction," "Romances," "Mysteries," etc.

- Not classifying periodicals; instead, arranging them alphabetically by title in a separate "Periodicals" section.

- Not classifying individual biographies; instead, arranging them alphabetically by the subjects' surnames in a separate "Biography" section.

- Using cutter letters instead of cutter numbers.

- Obtaining cutter numbers from cutter tables instead of synthesizing them from the Library of Congress's cuttering rules.

5. *Tracings* (subject headings and added entries/access points): General libraries with small collections catering mainly to students, novices, and casual readers may find that numerous tracings—long lists of subject headings and added entries—offer too much unnecessary information to patrons. Instead of making the local catalog a better and more informative research tool, the unwanted tracings clutter things up and

make searches more difficult or confusing. Eliminating unwanted tracings requires editing but slows down the growth of the catalog.

Decisions about these and other matters dictate what should and should not be included in local catalog records and how the information should appear. These decisions are important to make before choosing a source database and starting to do copy cataloging. Local variations that cannot be shown to have clear and tangible benefits for patrons should be avoided, because they take more editing time and, therefore, add to the cost a local library ends up paying for cataloging.

Overview of the Operation

Copy cataloging begins with choosing the source or sources for cataloging copy. Once sources are chosen, the operation involves the following steps: (1) searching and retrieving records to copy; (2) confirming the matches with the material to be cataloged; (3) editing data in the source record; (4) entering local data; and (5) producing the record.

Choosing the Source(s): Using Cataloging-in-Publication (CIP): One immediate advantage of CIP is that it appears in the material to be cataloged. Usually, a copy cataloger does not have to go beyond the material itself to find the CIP, although in some materials the CIP record is not reproduced in full and only a record number is given. Another advantage is that CIP information is prepared by knowledgeable catalogers and classifiers at the Library and Archives of Canada, the Library of Congress, or the British Library, whose work is the best in their respective nations.

1. *Searching and retrieving copy from source databases*: Copy catalogers are bound both by network contracts and by duty to search thoroughly for preexisting records that match their materials before entering original catalog records. The idea is to find existing records to copy, and good search techniques save more time, perhaps, than almost any other step of the copy cataloging process.

   The best search request is one likely to match only a desired title and no others. In other words, the ideal requested element relates to one title in the database. This type of element is called a "unique identifier," and several of these are given routinely in catalog records, among them the International Standard Book Numbers (ISBNs) or Library of Congress Control Numbers (LCCNs).

   When unique identifiers are absent from material being cataloged or when they fail to return matching records, other search options must be tried. These include titles proper and uniform titles, the names of personal and corporate body authors, and series titles. Of these options, titles proper are most efficient, followed by the names of authors or series titles. Uniform titles might be necessary to search if the material being cataloged has one. Combinations of names and titles are even better than titles alone or names alone. However, all these elements can be expected to match multiple titles in the database and are less efficient than unique identifiers.

2. *Confirming record matches and selecting a source record*: Once one or more source records are identified as possible matches, the copy cataloger must confirm an appropriate match. For example, if you are working with the OCLC database, the elements to be checked against the material in hand being cataloged include the type fixed field (for the format), date fixed field, title statement, edition, publisher, and physical description. If all these match the material, the record is likely to be a

good match. If more than one record is a full match to these fields, the "best" source record should be selected, defined as the one most likely to contain full, high-quality data (a national library record, a PCC library record, or a well-reputed network member, in that order).

Multiple matches sometimes include more than one national library record. In this event, it is preferable to use the record contributed by the one in the cataloger's home country.

Sometimes matches are not complete but are still useful. If a partial match contains the correct headings and title statements (for example, if the record is for a different edition of the same book) or differs in one or a few subelements (for example, if the record has the same title statement, but names a different publisher), it can still be chosen and edited to correct the data that differs from the material in hand. When a partial match is finally produced, however, the copy cataloger must know whether the edited record should be cloned into a new record (permissible if it is, indeed, a record for a different material) or merely added to the original source record.

3. *Editing the source records*: Call numbers are most likely to require editing. Some local libraries routinely assign their own call numbers, using the source data merely for guidance. If local library policy is to accept national library classification numbers, shelf marks may still have to be edited, unless they also are accepted as assigned. Library of Congress records do not provide shelf marks for Dewey call numbers, so these must be added. (Some libraries copy the shelf marks appearing in subfield b of the LC call number field.) Small libraries using Dewey call numbers might accept only the basic classification number but no expansions, or might accept only one expansion. Copy catalogers should be clear about policies governing both classification numbers and shelf marks.

Standard numbers and binding data in source records might differ from materials being cataloged if, for example, the source record was for a hardcover version of a title and the material in hand is a paperback, or *vice versa*. Both kinds of information may appear in the source record, but the local library chooses to accept only the data that matches its material. In either instance, copy catalogers must edit the appropriate field.

Information missing from source records entered as CIP, minimal level cataloging, or order records should be added. Sometimes this means only adding data in the physical description field, but at other times more is needed, including subject headings and added entries. If standard numbers, subtitles, statements of responsibility, series, important notes, and other useful data are missing from the source record, local library policies can be to add or ignore them. Editing policy should state clearly which fields should be added, if the information is available, and which should be ignored.

Similarly, errors in the source records might need to be corrected. Although some level of error can be tolerated in the interests of speeding up the process and saving money, data used by local library patrons should be corrected the first time the record is used, not at a later time after problems occur. It is less expensive to make desired changes at once than to wait and revise records later. Editing policy should state clearly which fields should be corrected if information in source records is wrong. At the very least, it seems sensible to correct errors in headings and other searchable fields.

4. *Entering local data*: In addition to call numbers, other local information relating to newly acquired materials needs to be added before the records can be considered complete. A note about a strictly local matter might be added to notes or tracings, for example, the fact that an author was the mayor from 1955 to 1958 or that a particular chapter contains information about the town's history (a note and an added subject heading). A whole category of library-specific data includes acquisitions data (vendors from whom materials are purchased, prices, dates of order and delivery, funds to which they are charged, names of requesters, etc.) and circulation data (the call numbers, copy numbers, loan types, etc.). Much of this data is copy-specific and does not normally appear on public catalog screen displays for patrons, although staff members can request it.

5. *Producing the records*: The final step in the process is producing completed records containing all the edited information desired by the local library for its catalog and other bibliographic files. When local records are uploaded to the database, the local libraries' identifications are added to the lists of holding libraries to show they own one or more copies of the cataloged materials. This information will be used by interlibrary loan librarians who seek to borrow copies of the materials for their patrons.

Unless a local library is permitted to make permanent changes to the records contributed by other libraries, the local edits do not alter or update the source records. When corrections are needed for the source records, copy catalogers should file correction reports with the source database quality control group so their records can be updated.

Summary

This chapter has covered the policies and procedures involved in cataloging materials by using existing catalog records as source copy instead of starting from scratch and building a complete new record for each material acquired by the library. Many catalogers, particularly in libraries buying mainstream materials likely to be cataloged before publication by national libraries, are accustomed to using CIP as source copy. This is the most basic kind of copy cataloging. It is just one step further to utilize other types of source copy, such as the catalog records contributed by members to bibliographic network databases.

CIP records are also part of bibliographic network databases, where, in time, they are routinely upgraded with data that cannot be obtained before publication, such as the number of pages in a book. National library records are a valuable source of cataloging copy. In addition, many librarians use records that are contributed to network databases by members doing original cataloging in their public, college, or university libraries. School library media centers and specialized information centers also contribute original catalog records to these networks, although they are fewer in number than other types of members. Bibliographic networks also share data among themselves, tape-loading batches of records into their databases. Tape loads can involve losing data in the transfer process and, as a result, may furnish less complete records than those contributed by means of direct uploads from the contributing libraries.

Issues that bear careful consideration are the sources a library accepts, the kind of editing done, and the amount of editing source records require before data can be entered into the local library catalog. A whole range of options exists, from no editing to complete editing of every element that differs from data that would have been recorded had the local library done original cataloging. The trade-off in setting local policies is that doing no editing is quickest and cheapest, but maximizes the number of errors in the local catalog, while doing complete editing takes longest and is most expensive, but maximizes the purity and integrity of the local catalog.

Most catalogers make decisions that strike a compromise between no editing and perfect editing—for example, editing only those fields likely to affect retrieval or cause major confusion for searchers. At the same time, they try to find the best possible records to copy, which are contributed by libraries known for doing high-quality original work. The best safeguard of a local library's catalog is having knowledgeable copy catalogers who recognize the difference between major and minor issues, and who, themselves, do high-quality copy cataloging.

Additional Information

Appendix: Answers to Exercises

CHAPTER 3

Answer to Exercise 3A

This example is an illustration of:

- other title information (in 2nd level cataloging)
- detailed pagination
- bibliography note (in 2nd level cataloging)
- two ISBNs noted
- Library of Congress CIP
- two levels of cataloging

1st level cataloging

```
Barham, Andrea.
   The pedant's revolt. -- Delacourt, 2006.
   xii, 148 p.

   ISBN-10 0-385-34016-8.
   ISBN-13 978-0-385-34016-8.
```

2nd level cataloging

```
Barham, Andrea.
   The pedant's revolt : know what know-it-alls know / Andrea Barham. -
New York : Delacourt, 2006.
   xii, 148 p. : ill. ; 19 cm.

   Includes bibliographical references.
   ISBN-10 0-385-34016-8.
   ISBN-13 978-0-385-34016-8.
```

Answer to Exercise 3B

This example is an illustration of:

- subsidiary responsibility (in 2nd level cataloging)
- detailed pagination statement
- colored illustrations
- index note (in 2nd level cataloging)
- British Library CIP
- two levels of cataloging

1st level cataloging

Severin, Tim.
  In search of Genghis Khan. -- Hutchinson, 1991.
  ix, 276 p., [32] p. of plates.

  ISBN 0-09-174779-1.

2nd level cataloging

Severin, Tim.
  In search of Genghis Khan / by Tim Severin ; photographs by Paul
Harris. -- London : Hutchinson, 1991.
  ix, 276 p., [32] p. of plates : ill. (some col.) ; 24 cm.

  Includes index.
  ISBN 0-09-174779-1.

Answer to Exercise 3C

This example is an illustration of:

- other title information (in 2nd level cataloging)
- detailed pagination
- descriptive illustration statement (in 2nd level cataloging)
- publication date not listed, copyright date given
- bibliography and index note with page numbers of bibliography noted (in 2nd level cataloging)
- two ISBNs qualified
- Library of Congress CIP's other title information incorrect
- two levels of cataloging

1st level cataloging

O'Shea, Stephen.
  Sea of faith. -- Walker, c2006.
  xii, 411 p.

  ISBN-13 978-0-8027-1498-5 (hardcover).
  ISBN-10 0-8027-1498-6 (hardcover).

2nd level cataloging

O'Shea, Stephen.
  Sea of faith : Islam and Christianity in the medieval Mediterranean
world / Stephen O'Shea. -- New York : Walker, c2006.
  xii, 411 p. : ill., maps, ports. ; 24 cm.

  Includes bibliographical references (p. [385]-394) and index.

  ISBN-13 978-0-8027-1498-5 (hardcover).
  ISBN-10 0-8027-1498-6 (hardcover).

Answer to Exercise 3D

This example is an illustration of:

- other title information (in 2nd level cataloging)
- edition statement (in 2nd level cataloging)
- publication date not listed, copyright date given
- detailed pagination
- bibliography note (in 2nd level cataloging)
- two levels of cataloging

1st level cataloging

```
Truss, Lynne.
  Eats, shoots & leaves. -- Gotham Books, c2004.
  xxvii, 209 p.

  ISBN 1-592-40087-6.
```

2nd level cataloging

```
Truss, Lynne.
  Eats, shoots & leaves : the zero tolerance approach to punctuation /
Lynne Truss. -- 1st American ed. -- New York : Gotham Books, c2004.
  xxvii, 209 p. ; 20 cm.

  Includes bibliographical references.
  ISBN 1-592-40087-6.
```

Publication statement for a Canadian library:

New York ; Toronto : Gotham Books, c2004.

CHAPTER 4

Answer to Exercise 4A

This example is an illustration of:

- joint authors
- other title information (in 2nd level cataloging)
- distributor
- descriptive illustration statement (in 2nd level cataloging)
- bibliography note (in 2nd level cataloging)
- personal name added entry
- title added entry
- British Library CIP
- two levels of cataloging

1st level cataloging

Pankhurst, Richard.
  Ethiopia photographed / Richard Pankhurst & Denis Gérard. -- Kegan
Paul, 1996.
  168 p.

  ISBN 0-7103-0504-4.

  I. Gérard, Denis. II. Title.

2nd level cataloging

Pankhurst, Richard.
  Ethiopia photographed : historic portraits of the country and its
people taken between 1867 and 1935 / Richard Pankhurst & Denis Gérard.
-- London : Kegan Paul, 1996.
  168 p. : mostly ill. ; 29 cm.

  Includes bibliographical references.
  ISBN 0-7103-0504-4.

I. Gérard, Denis. II. Title.

In cataloging for a U.S. library, the publication distribution
statement would be:

London : Kegan Paul ; New York : Columbia University Press
[distributor], 1996.

Answer to Exercise 4B

This example is an illustration of:

- edited work entered under title
- detailed pagination
- series statement(in 2nd level cataloging) not traced
- bibliography and index note (in 2nd level cataloging)
- ISBN qualified
- added entry for editor (form of name taken from the established form in the Library of Congress CIP)

1st level cataloging

Cross-cultural perspectives on knowledge management / edited by
   David J. Pauleen. -- Libraries Unlimited, 2007.
   xix, 259 p.

   ISBN 1-59158-331-4 (alk. paper).

   I. Pauleen, David.

2nd level cataloging

Cross-cultural perspectives on knowledge management / edited by
   David J. Pauleen. -- Westport, Conn. : Libraries Unlimited,
   2007.
   xix, 259 p. ; 23 cm. -- (Libraries Unlimited knowledge management
series)

   Includes bibliographical references and index.
   ISBN 1-59158-331-4 (alk. paper).

   I. Pauleen, David.

Answer to Exercise 4C

This example is an illustration of:

- joint authors
- other title information (in 2nd level cataloging)
- publishing date not listed; copyright date given
- detailed pagination
- bibliography note (in 2nd level cataloging)
- personal name added entry
- title added entry
- two levels of cataloging

1st level cataloging

Jenkins, Susan.
  Life signs / Susan Jenkins and Robert Jenkins. -- Harper Collins,
c1998.
  xiii, 189 p.

  ISBN 0-06-019154-6.

  I. Jenkins, Robert.   II. Title.

2nd level cataloging

Jenkins, Susan.
  Life signs : the biology of Star trek / Susan Jenkins and Robert
Jenkins. -- New York : Harper Collins, c1998.
  xiii, 189 p. : ill. ; 24 cm.

  Includes bibliographical references.
  ISBN 0-06-019154-6.

  I. Jenkins, Robert.   II. Title.

Note that the "S" in Star trek is capitalized because it is the first
word in another title.

Answer to Exercise 4D

This example is an illustration of:

- catalog records with and without a uniform title
- main entry/access point from title proper
- subsidiary responsibility statement
- personal name added entry with optional designation of function
- title added entry

2nd level cataloging without a uniform title (suitable for general collections)

Shaw, Bernard.
   The sayings of Bernard Shaw / edited by Joseph Spence. -- London :
Duckworth, 1993.
   64 p. ; 20 cm.

   ISBN 0-7156-2491-1.

   I. Spence, Joseph, ed.   II. Title.

2nd level cataloging with a uniform title (suitable for large collections of Shaw's works)

Shaw, Bernard.
   [Selections]
   The sayings of Bernard Shaw / edited by Joseph Spence. -- London :
Duckworth, 1993.
   64 p. ; 20 cm.

   ISBN 0-7156-2491-1.

I. Spence, Joseph, ed.   II. Title.

CHAPTER 5

Answers to Exercise 5A

Figure 2.1: Subject heading # 1 should be 1. Errors.

Figure 3.2: Same.

Figure 3.5: Subject headings #1, #2, and #4 same; #3 should be 3. Literature.

Exercise 3C: Subdivision in Sears is "Military history;" subject heading #1 "Mediterranean Region" is not in Sears, but is acceptable because it is a geographic name; "Islamic Empire" is not in Sears and "Islamic countries" is not really the same as "Islamic Empire," but could be retained if considered on the same level as the name of a country. Subject headings #3 and #4 are the same. Therefore, retain all the CIP subject headings with the only change being to have the subdivisions in subject headings #1, #2, and #3 " — Military history."

Figure 4.1: Subject heading #1 same; #2 should be 2. Mosquitoes — Control.

Figure 4.2: Subject headings #2 and #3 same; #1 should be deleted because there is no Sears equivalent.

Figure 4.3: Same.

Figure 4.4: LCSH too specific for Sears; #1 should be 1. Motion pictures.

Figure 4.5: The very specific LCSH headings are difficult to translate into Sears headings. Suggested tracing: 1. Serial publications — Conference proceedings. 2. Libraries — Special collections — Serial publications — Conference proceedings. 3. Electronic publishing — Conference proceedings, and possibly going beyond Sears Rule of Three. 4. Library science — Conference proceedings.

Figure 4.6: Subject headings #2, #3, and #4 same; #1 should be 1. Eating customs. A small library might need only 1. Eating customs. 2. Food.

Figure 4.7: Same. However, with the Sears Rule of Three, a cataloger would need to examine the book's content to determine which three of these subject headings to eliminate.

Exercise 4B: Same.

Answer to Exercise 5B

This example is an illustration of:

- other title information (in 2nd level cataloging)
- subsidiary responsibility (in 2nd level cataloging)
- detailed pagination
- descriptive illustration statement (in 2nd level cataloging)
- index note (in 2nd level cataloging)
- two ISBNs qualified
- personal name added entry
- title added entry
- comparison of Sears and Library of Congress Subject headings
- Library and Archives of Canada CIP with incorrect other title information
- two levels of cataloging

1st level cataloging with Sears subject headings

Ebadi, Shirin.
  Iran awakening / Shirin Ebadi ; with Azadeh Moaveni. -- Knopf, 2006.
  xvi, 232 p.

  ISBN-13 978-0-676-97802-5 (bound).
  ISBN-10 0-676-97802-9 (bound).

  1. Edadi, Shirin. 2. Human rights workers -- Iran. 3. Women lawyers -- Iran. 4. Women -- Iran -- Social conditions. 5. Iran -- Politics and government. I. Moaveni, Azadeh. II. Title.

2nd level cataloging with Library of Congress subject headings

Ebadi, Shirin.
  Iran awakening : from prison to peace prize : one woman's struggle at the crossroads of history / Shirin Ebadi ; with Azadeh Moaveni. -- Toronto : Knopf, 2006.
  xvi, 232 p. : ill., maps, ports. ; 25 cm.

  Includes index.
  ISBN-13 978-0-676-97802-5 (bound).
  ISBN-10 0-676-97802-9 (bound).

  1. Ebadi, Shirin. 2. Women human rights workers -- Iran. 3. Women lawyers -- Iran. 4. Women -- Iran -- Social conditions. 5. Iran -- Politics and government -- 1979-1997. I. Moaveni, Azadeh. II. Title.

Note: The publication/distribution statement for this book in a U.S. library would be:

Toronto : Knopf ; New York : Random House, 2006.

Answer to Exercise 5C

This example is an illustration of:

- fiction book
- ISBN qualified
- Library of Congress and Sears subject headings the same
- title added entry
- two levels of cataloging

1st level cataloging

Truong, Monique.
  The book of salt. -- Vintage, 2004.
  261 p.

  ISBN 0-09-945545-5 (pbk).

  1. Stein, Gertrude -- Fiction. 2. Toklas, Alice B. -- Fiction.
I. Title.

2nd level cataloging

Truong, Monique.
  The book of salt / Monique Truong. -- London : Vintage, 2004.
  261 p. ; 20 cm.

  ISBN 0-09-945545-5 (pbk).

  1. Stein, Gertrude -- Fiction. 2. Toklas, Alice B. -- Fiction.
I. Title.

———————

Answer To Exercise 5D

This example is an illustration of:

- compiled work entered under title
- date of publication unknown
- length of item less than width (in 2nd level cataloging)
- index note (in 2nd level cataloging)
- Sears subject heading and Library of Congress subject headings compared
- added entry for compiler
- two levels of cataloging

1st level cataloging with Sears subject headings

Scottish country recipes / compiled by Johanna Mathie. Salmon,
   [19--?]
   47 p.

   ISBN 1-902842-21-9.

   1. Scottish cooking. I. Mathie, Johanna.

2nd level cataloging with Library of Congress subject headings

Scottish country recipes / compiled by Johanna Mathie ;
   illustrations by H.J. Dobson. -- Sevenoaks, England : Salmon,
   [19--?]
   47 p. : ill. ; 12 x 17 cm.

   Includes index.
   ISBN 1-902842-21-9.

   1. Cookery, Scottish. I. Mathie, Johanna.

Answer to Exercise 5E

This example is an illustration of:

- nonfiction book for young readers
- bibliographic form of author's name taken from CIP record
- other title information
- publication dated not listed; copyright date given
- length of book longer than height
- bibliography and index note; book includes an index that was not noted in the CIP record
- summary
- title added entry
- Library of Congress CIP with Library of Congress subject headings and AC subject headings for young readers
- 2nd level cataloging for an adult collection and for a children's collection

2nd level cataloging for an adult collection

Carlson, Laurie M.
  Classical kids : an activity guide to life in ancient Greece and Rome
/ Laurie Carlson. -- Chicago : Chicago Review Press, c1998.
  186 p. : ill. ; 22 x 28 cm.

  Includes bibliographic references and index.
  Summary: Demonstrates life in ancient Greece and Rome, and the
contribution of those cultures to modern civilization, through hands-on
activities such as making a star gazer, chiselling a clay tablet, and
weaving Roman sandals.
  ISBN 1-55652-290-8.

  1. Greece -- Social life and customs -- Juvenile literature. 2. Rome
-- Social life and customs -- Juvenile literature. 3. Creative
activities and seat work -- Juvenile literature. I. Title.

2nd level cataloging for a children's collection

Carlson, Laurie M.
  Classical kids : an activity guide to life in ancient Greece and Rome
/ Laurie Carlson. -- Chicago : Chicago Review Press, c1998.
  186 p. : ill. ; 22 x 28 cm.

  Summary: Demonstrates life in ancient Greece and Rome, and the
contribution of those cultures to modern civilization, through hands-on
activities such as making a star gazer, chiselling a clay tablet, and
weaving Roman sandals.
  ISBN 1-55652-290-8.

  1. Greece -- Civilization To 146 B.C. 2. Rome -- Civilization.
3. Handicraft. I. Title.

Note: In the CIP the capital "A" on "Ancient Greece" is incorrect
because there is no geographic name "Ancient Greece." The correct
capitalization is found in the summary note.

Answers to Exercise 5F

Recipes for cooking with chocolate

1. Cookery (Chocolate)   (LCSH)

1. Cooking — Chocolate (Sears)

Immigration: an issue for our times

1. Emigration and immigration (LCSH)

1. Immigration and emigration (Sears)

Coping with business recessions

1. Recessions — Psychological aspects. 2. Recessions — Health aspects. (LCSH)

2. Same two subject headings (Sears)

Museums in Vancouver, BC

1. Museums — British Columbia — Vancouver (LCSH)

1. Museums — Vancouver (BC) (Sears)

Aids to geographical research (a list of books and periodicals)

1. Geography — Bibliography. 2. Geography — Periodicals — Bibliography. (LCSH)

2. Same two subject headings (Sears)

Psychology applied to industry

1. Psychology, Industrial. (LCSH)

1. Industries — Psychological aspects. (Sears)

The fight for women's suffrage in England

1. Women — Suffrage — England (LCSH)

2. Same subject heading (Sears)

The ancient Japanese art of paper folding

1. Origami (LCSH)

2. Same subject heading (Sears)

Air conditioning and refrigeration

1. Air conditioning. 2. Refrigeration and refrigeration machinery. (LCSH)

1. Same subject heading. 2. Refrigeration. (Sears)

A pop-up book of farm animals in Montana

1. Livestock — Montana. 2. Toy and movable books. (LCSH)

1. Domestic animals — Montana. 2. Same subject heading. (Sears)

Recent exhibitions of postimpressionist art

1. Post-impressionism (Art) — Exhibitions (LCSH)

2. Postimpressionism (Art) — Exhibitions (Sears)

Answers to Exercise 5G

1. Free trade — Canada. 2. Free trade — United States. 3. Canada — Commerce — United States. 4. United States — Commerce — Canada. 5. Canada — Commercial policy — United States. 6. United States — Commercial policy — Canada. (LCSH)

Sears has the same headings for #1 and #2. 3. Canada — Commerce. 4. United States — Commerce. 5. Commercial policy — Canada. 6. Commercial policy — United States.

Answers to Exercise 5H

A book of pictures about the War of 1812 on Canadian soil

1. Canada — History — War of 1812 — Pictorial works

Note: "Pictorial works" taken from LCSH list of subdivisions

Battle of Batoche in Saskatchewan

1. Batoche, Battle of, Batoche, Sask., 1885

The massacre of women students at the Ecole Polytechnique in Montreal

1. Montréal École Polytechnique Women Students Massacre, Montréal, Québec, 1969

CHAPTER 6

Answers to Exercise 6A

(i) Because the twenty-second edition of DDC was published in 2003, classification numbers need to be checked if the book was published before that date. DDCs assigned in 2003 should also be checked if there is reason to believe that the DDCs were assigned early in the year before DDC22's publication.

(ii) The figures/exercises whose DDC number should be checked in DDC22 are figures 2.1, 2.3, 4.1, 4.3, 4.5, 4.6, 4.7, and Exercise 4A.

(iii) None of these DDC numbers needed to be changed.

Answer to Exercise 6B

Numbers from Table 1 and Table 2 are never used alone and may be used with any number unless this is expressly forbidden in the DDC schedules. Table 1 lists standard subdivisions; Table 2 is used where appropriate to indicate geographic areas or biographic treatment.

Answers to Exercise 6C

6 = Technology (Applied sciences)

68 = Manufacture of products for specific uses

686 = Printing and related activities

686.2 = Printing

686.23 = Presswork (Impression)

686.232 = Photomechanical techniques

686.2327 = Photoengraving (Photointaglio)

686.232705 = a periodical about photoengraving

Answer to Exercise 6D

599.665 would be assigned to a book about horses as zoological animals and 636.1 would be assigned to a book about horses as domestic animals.

Answer to Exercise 6E

956.7 is assigned to a history of Iraq, while 915.67 is assigned to the geography of, or travel in, modern Iraq.

Answers to Exercise 6F

A book about foreign relations between the United States and Canada.

(i) if the book were housed in a U.S. library, 327.73071

(ii) if the book were housed in a Canadian library, 327.71073

Answers to Exercise 6G

The following classification numbers have been selected from the unabridged DDC. If the numbers from the abridged DDC differ, those numbers are enclosed in parentheses. DDC numbers are sometimes difficult to find in the abridged DDC because specific subjects are not included under some subjects.

(a) field hockey	796.355
(b) divorce mediation	306.89
(c) descriptive cataloging	025.32 (025.3)
(d) understanding acute leukemia	616.994.19 (616.99)
(e) winter Olympic games	796.98
(f) Royal Canadian Mounted Police	363.20971
(g) space walks	629.4584 (629.45)
(h) insurance against earthquakes	368.1226 (368.1)
(i) Hinduism	294.5
(j) a journal of physics	530.05
(k) life expectancy in China	304.64531 (304.6)
(l) museums in Cleveland	069.0977132 (069.09771)
(m) a history of the education of women	371.82209
(n) picture book of church buildings	726.50222 (726.5022)
(o) Great Barrier Reef, Australia	919.43
(p) collection of humorous riddles	808.882 (808.88)
(q) legendary heroes	398.22
(r) medical dictionary of substance abuse	616.8603
(s) distance education in Winnipeg	371.3509712743 (371.35097127)
(t) design of fire escapes	628.922 (628.9)

Answer to Exercise 6H

This example is an illustration of:

- other title information (in 2nd level cataloging)
- detailed pagination
- series (in 2nd level cataloging)
- glossary and index note
- title added entry
- series added entry (in 2nd level cataloging)
- comparison of Sears and LCSH
- comparison of abridged and unabridged DDC (in this instance, no difference)
- partial contents note
- two levels of cataloging

1st level cataloging with Sears subject headings and abridged DDC

Ebbutt, M.I.
  The British. -- Bracken, c1985.
  [13], 374 p., [64] p. of plates.

  ISBN 0-946495-83-1.

  1. Legends -- Great Britain. 2. Folklore -- Great Britain.
3. Mythology, British. I. Title.

Abridged DDC: 398.2041

2nd level cataloging with LCSH and unabridged DDC

Ebbutt, M.I.
  The British / M.I. Ebbutt ; with illustrations from drawings and famous paintings. -- London : Bracken, c1985.
  [13], 374 p., [64] p. of plates : ill. ; 23 cm. -- (Myths and legends series)

  Includes glossary and index.
  ISBN 0-946495-83-1.

  1. Legends -- Great Britain. 2. Folklore -- Great Britain.
3. British mythology. I. Title. II. Series.

Unabridged DDC: 398.2041

Note: Although the statement of extent is correct according to AACR2, it is likely that a library using 1st level cataloging would reduce the extent statement to "374 p."

Each of this book's thirteen chapters is devoted to one person. The library may choose to give a partial contents note to certain of these people, such as Beowulf and Robin Hood, and to give them an added entry. The contents note would be:
  Partial contents: Beowulf -- Robin Hood.

CHAPTER 7

Answer to Exercise 7A

This example is an illustration of:

- fiction book (although the MARC format declares 090 obsolete, it is used by some libraries when the call number does not include a classification number; other libraries use 082 for the DDC and 090 for the library's call number)
- other title information
- separate sequences of pagination
- contents note
- two ISBNs with qualifications listed on verso; pertinent one given in bibliographic record
- Library of Congress subject headings
- title added entry
- Library of Congress CIP
- 2nd level cataloging

```
020      $a 0594200440 (pbk).
090      $a Fic $b BRO
100 1    $a Brooks, Geraldine.
245 10   $a March : $a novel / $c Geraldine Brooks.
260      $a New York : $b Penguin Books, $c 2006.
300      $a 280, 3, 9 p. ; $c 20 cm.
504      $a Questions for discussion: p. 8-9 at end of book.
586      $a Pulitzer Prize winner.
650   0  $a March family (Fictitious characters) $x Fiction.
650   0  $a Fathers and daughters $x Fiction.
650   0  $a Soldiers $x Fiction.
651   0  $a United States $x History $y Civil War, 1861-1865 $x Fiction.
```

Notes:
The publication/distribution area in a Canadian catalog would read:

```
260      $a New York ; Toronto : $b Penguin Books, $c 2006.
```

Additional notes about the book being a Pulitzer Prize winner may be of interest to readers and the questions for discussion to book groups.

Answer to Exercise 7B

This example is an illustration of:

- fiction book (compare the 090 tag with Exercise 7A; $b in this exercise has a cutter number)
- uniform title
- subsidiary responsibility
- edition statement
- edition and history note
- added entry for translator with optional designation of function
- Library of Congress subject headings
- ISBN qualified
- title added entry
- additional title added
- Library of Congress CIP
- 2nd level cataloging

```
020     $a 0060740450 (softcover).
090     $a Fic $b G165
100 1   $a García Márquez, Gabriel.
240 10  $a Cien años de soledad. [$l English]
245 10  $a One hundred years of solitude / $c Gabriel García Márquez ;
translated from the Spanish by Gregory Rabassa.
250     $a 1st perennial classics ed.
260     $a New York : $b Perennial Classics, $c 1998.
300     $a 458 p. ; $c 21 cm.
500     $a Originally published in 1970.
650  0  $a Epic literature.
651  0  $a Macondo (Imaginary place)$x Fiction.
651  0  $a Latin America $x Social conditions $x Fiction.
700 1   $a Rabassa, Gregory, $e tr.
```

Answer to Exercise 7C

This example is an illustration of:

- unabridged Dewey decimal classification with shelf mark
- other title information
- detailed pagination
- descriptive illustration statement
- quoted note
- contents (bibliography)note
- Library of Congress subject headings
- title added entry
- DDC different than one listed in Library of Congress CIP
- 2nd level cataloging

```
020     $a 0156716607.
082 04 $a 970.498 $b B633 $2 22.
100 1  $a Boeri, David.
245 10 $a People of the ice whale : $b Eskimos, white men, and the
whale world / $c David Boeri.
260     $a San Diego : $b Harcourt Brace Jovanovich, $c 1983.
300     $a xvi, 285 p.: $b ill., maps ; $c 20 cm.
500     $a "A Harvest/HBJ book."
504     $a Includes bibliographical references.
650  0 $a Eskimos $z Alaska $x Fishing.
650  0 $a Indians if North America $z Alaska $x Fishing.
650  0 $a Whaling $z Alaska.
650  0 $a Bowhead whale.
650  0 $a Wildlife conservation $z Alaska.
```

Notes:
In 082, this alternative is allowed by DDC. Another possibility is
979.100498

The reprint statement in the Library of Congress CIP does not exist
elsewhere in the book, so it has not been added to the MARC record.

Answer to Exercise 7D

This example is an illustration of:

- unabridged DDC with shelf mark
- other title information
- publishing date not listed, copyright date given
- descriptive illustration statement
- quoted note
- bibliography and index note
- personal name subject headings
- Library of Congress subject headings
- title added entry
- Canadian CIP (from other than library and Archives of Canada)
- 2nd level cataloging

```
020    $a 00006386598.
082 04 $a 917.19041091 $b M177 $2 22.
100 1  $a McGoogan, Kenneth.
245 10 $a Fatal passage : $b the untold story of John Rae, the Arctic
explorer who discovered the fate of Franklin / $c Ken McGoogan.
260    $a Toronto : $b Harper Perennial Canada, $c c2001.
300    $a 327 p.: $b ill., map, ports. ; $c 23 cm.
500    $a "A Phyllis Bruce book."
504    $a Includes bibliographical references and index.
600 10 $a Rae, John.
600 10 $a Franklin, John, $c Sir.
650  0 $a Explorers $z Scotland $v Biography.
651  0 $a Arctic regions $x Discovery and exploration $x British.
651  0 $a Northwest, Canadian $x Discovery and exploration $x British.
651  0 $a Northwest passage $x Discovery and exploration $x British.
```

Answer to Exercise 7E

This example is an illustration of:

- abridged DDC with call letters
- other title information
- descriptive illustration statement
- bibliography and index note
- Sears subject headings
- title added entry
- Library of Congress CIP
- 2nd level cataloging

```
020     $a 1594489254.
082 14 $a 614.5 $b JOH $2 14.
100 1  $a Johnson, Steven.
245 14 $a The ghost map : $b the story of London's most terrifying
epidemic—and how it changed science, cities, and the modern world / $c
Steven Johnson.
260     $a New York : $b Riverhead Books, $c 2006.
300     $a 299 p. : $b ill., maps, ports. ; $c 24 cm.
504     $a Includes bibliographical references and index.
650   7 $a Cholera $z England $2 Sears.
651   7 $a London $x History $y 19th century $2 Sears.
```

Note: Sears does not permit the subject heading string found in LC's
CIP. Therefore, it has been broken into two Sears' subject headings.

Answer to Exercise 7F

This example is an illustration of:

- unabridged DDC with call letters
- edited work entered under title
- other title information
- word added to statement of responsibility
- subsidiary responsibility
- edition statement taken from outside chief sources
- detailed pagination
- descriptive illustration statement
- edition and history note
- added entries for editors
- Library of Congress subject headings
- 2nd level cataloging

```
020      $a 0349104972.
082 04 $a 954.03 $b PLA $2 22
245 00 $a Plain tales from the Raj : $b images of British India in the
twentieth century / $c edited [by] Charles Allen in association with
Michael Mason ; introduction by Philip Mason.
250      $a [New ed.]
260      $a London : $b Abacus, $c 2000.
300      $a 287 p., [8] p of plates : $b ill., facsims. ; $c 20 cm.
500      $a Originally published by Deutsch, 1975.
650  0 $a British $z India $x History $y 20th century.
651  0 $ India $x Description and travel.
700 1  $a Allen, Charles.
700 1  $a Mason, Michael.
```

Answer to Exercise 7G

This example is an illustration of:

- unabridged Dewey decimal classification with call letters
- primary statement of responsibility as part of the title proper
- edition statement
- distributor
- detailed pagination
- descriptive illustration statement
- Library of Congress subject heading
- title added entry
- additional title added entry
- 2nd level cataloging

```
020     $a 1566915198.
082 04 $a 438 $b STE $2 22.
100 1  $a Steves, Rick.
245 10 $a Rick Steve's German phrase book & dictionary.
246 10 $a German phrase book & dictionary.
350     $a 5th ed.
260     $a Emeryville, CA : $b Avalon Travel ; $a Berkeley, CA : $b
Publishers Group West [distributor], $c 2003.
300     $a xi, 279 p. : $b ill., maps ; $c 15 cm.
650  0 $a German language $v Conversation and phrase books $x English.
```

Note: Table 4 has not been discussed in this book, so the basic DDC number for the German language has not been expanded here to conform with the subject heading.

Answer to Exercise 7H

This example is an illustration of:

- complex DDC number with cutter number
- other title information
- detailed pagination
- descriptive illustration statement
- bibliography and index note
- Library of Congress subject heading
- title added entry
- 2nd level cataloging

```
020    $a 0786712279.
082 04 $a 328.45663940941 $b M872 $2 22.
100 1  $a Moxham, Roy.
245 10 $a Tea $b addiction, exploitation and empire / $c Roy Moxham.
260    $a New York : Carroll & Graf, $c 2003.
300    $a xii, 271 p. : $b ill., maps ; $c 22 cm.
504    $a Includes bibliographical references and index.
650  0 $a Tea trade $z Great Britain $x History.
```

Note: This complex DDC number may be difficult for beginning catalogers to construct.

382.4 (the base number for international commerce by products and services) instructs the cataloger to add numbers following 380.141-380.145. At this point, "5" is added to the base number = 382.45. At 380.145, the cataloger is further instructed for specific products and services to add from 001-999 (the whole DDC classification).

663.94 is the DDC number for tea. This number is added, making the DDC number 328.4566394.

0941 is the number for Great Britain in Table 1. When this is added, the DDC becomes 328.45663940941, which means British international trade in tea.

A number of this length would be used only in large collections.

————————————

Answer to Exercise 71

This example is an illustration of:

- unabridged Dewey decimal classification with call letters
- colophon as source of information
- joint authors
- word added to statement of responsibility to enhance meaning
- edition statement
- publishing date not listed; copyright date given
- descriptive illustration statement
- index note
- personal name added entry
- Library of Congress subject heading
- corporate body added entry
- title added entry
- 2nd level cataloging

```
020      $a 1566915198.
082 04   $a 914.39 $b FAL $2 22.
100 1    $a Fallon, Steve.
245 10   $a Hungary / $c Steve Fallon [and] Neal Bedford.
350      $a 5th ed.
260      $a Footscray, Vic. : Lonely Planet, $c c2006.
300      $a 424 p. : $b col. ill., maps ; $c 20 cm.
504      $a Includes index.
651  0   $a Hungary $v Guidebooks.
700 0    $a Bedford, Neal.
710 2    $a Lonely Planet Publications.
```

Note: Publishers are not normally given added entries. In this case, the added entry is made because Lonely Planet guidebooks are frequently sought by travellers.

———————

Answer to Exercise 7J

This example is an illustration of:

- unabridged DDC with call letters
- edited work entered under the title
- other title information
- subsidiary responsibility
- detailed pagination
- no illustrations
- index note
- added entries for the editor
- Sears subject headings
- two ISBNs
- 2nd level cataloging

```
020     $a 9780977861743.
020     $a 0977861740.
082 14 $a 027.473 $b LIB $2 14.
245 00 $a Library daylight : $b tracings of modern librarianship, 1874-
1922 / $c edited by Rory Litwin ; with an introduction by Suzanne
Stauffer.
260     $a Duluth, Minn. : $b Library Juice Press, $c 2006.
300     $a xiii, 248 p. ; $c 23 cm.
504     $a Includes index.
650  0 $a Library science $z United States $x History.
650  0 $a Public libraries $z United States $x History.
700  1 $a Litwin, Rory.
```

Note: AACR-2005 directs a cataloger not to include "Dr." in a statement
of responsibility.

———————————

Glossary

This list of acronyms and cataloging terms includes those defined in the text and some terms not used in the text, but often encountered in the cataloging literature.

AACR. *Anglo-American Cataloguing Rules*. Cataloging rules cooperatively developed by the library associations and national libraries of the United States, the United Kingdom, Canada, and, beginning in 1981, Australia.

AACR2. *Anglo-American Cataloguing Rules*, 1978. The second edition of AACR, this time published in one version for all the participating nations.

AACR2-2005. *Anglo-American Cataloguing Rules*, second edition, 2002 revision, with updates issued in 2003, 2004, and 2005. This is the current version of descriptive cataloging rules at this writing.

AC heading. Annotated card heading. Subject heading from a special list of terms created for the Library of Congress for juvenile materials. *See also* Annotated card program.

Access. The process of choosing and formulating headings for bibliographic records. Also refers to the larger processes of providing bibliographic access (that is, cataloging), intellectual access (that is, classification and indexing), and physical access to material.

Access point. Any name, word, or phrase by which a catalog record can be retrieved from the catalog, known also as an *entry*, *heading*, or *retrieval point*.

Added entry. A secondary access point; any heading by which a catalog record can be retrieved other than the first (or *main*) entry.

ALA. American Library Association.

ALCTS. Association for Library Collections & Technical Services. A division of the American Library Association called the Resources and Technical Services Division before 1989.

Alternative title. A title following the title proper and preceded by the word "or," in any language. For example, the underlined data in the operetta by Gilbert and Sullivan titled: *Trial by jury, or, The lass who loved a sailor*.

AMICUS. The resource-sharing database of the Library and Archives of Canada.

Analytic(s). Catalog records or access points for a work that is part of a larger bibliographic unit, for example, one play in a book containing several plays.

Annotated Card Program. Program initiated by the Library of Congress for cataloging juvenile materials that includes adding specialized subject headings and summary notes to the catalog records.

Area of description. One of the eight parts of a bibliographic description designated by ISBD and AACR2-2005, for example, the edition area (area 2) or the series area (area 6).

Authority file. A file containing the official forms of names, uniform titles, series titles, subject headings, or all used as access points in a library catalog, and citations to sources used to establish them as well as cross-references to variant forms.

Authority record. One record in an authority file. *See also* name authority, subject authority.

Auxiliary table. In classification, a separate table of subdivisions intended to be used with numbers from the main schedules.

Bibliographic description. The part of a catalog record that identifies the item it represents, exclusive of access points, call numbers, and other control numbers other than the ISBN.

Bibliographic identity. The name used on an item to identify the creator. One who uses more than one name on his or her works is said to have multiple bibliographic identities.

Bibliographic level. One of three standard styles of description prescribed by AACR2-2005, each containing varying amounts of bibliographic information from the least (level 1) to the most (level 3).

Bibliographic network. A group of libraries that shares a computerized database of bibliographic information or whose individual bibliographic databases are electronically linked.

Bibliographic record. A catalog record.

Bibliographic unit. A cataloging unit; an entity capable of being cataloged, indexed, and classified, such as a book or other formats in a library's collection.

Bibliographic utility. A group of electronically linked libraries that generates new catalog records.

Blind reference. A cross-reference used in a catalog that leads searchers to a term having no entries under it.

Book mark. *See* Cutter number, Shelf mark.

Book number. *See* Cutter number, Shelf mark.

Boolean operators. The words AND, OR, NOT, etc., used in combining subject terms for retrieval.

Boolean retrieval. Computer programs based on Boolean algebra that permit retrieval for combinations of search terms.

Call letter. *See* Shelf mark.

Call number. The shelf address of an item, usually consisting of its classification number and shelf marks.

Canadian Committee on Cataloguing. A member of the Joint Steering Committee for Revision of AACR that was responsible for *AACR2-2005* and a member of the Joint Steering Committee for Development of RDA that is responsible for *Resource Description and Access*.

Canadian Subject Headings. A list of subject headings suitable for Canadian materials; published by the Library and Archives of Canada.

Cataloging Distribution Service. The marketing agency for the Library of Congress's bibliographic products.

Cataloging Service Bulletin. A Library of Congress periodical publication providing news of cataloging policy decisions, new subject authorities, etc.

CCC. *See* Canadian Committee on Cataloguing.

CC:DA. Committee on Cataloging: Description and Access, a committee of the Cataloging and Classification Section of the Association for Library Collections & Technical Services, a division of the American Library Association. This committee is member of the Joint Steering Committee for Revision of AACR that was responsible for *AACR2-2005* and a member of the Joint Steering Committee for Development of RDA that is responsible for *Resource Description and Access*.

CDS. *See* Cataloging Distribution Service.

Chartered Institute of Library and Information Professionals. Formerly known as the Library Association, a professional association for librarians and information specialists in the United Kingdom and a member of the Joint Steering Committee for Revision of AACR that was responsible for *AACR2-2005* and a member of the Joint Steering Committee for Development of RDA that is responsible for *Resource Description and Access*.

Chief source. In descriptive cataloging, the main location from which bibliographic data are taken, such as the title page of a book, title screens of an electronic resource, etc. *See also* Prescribed source.

CILIP. *See* Chartered Institute of Library and Information Professionals.

Citation order. In classification and indexing, a prescribed order in which the components of a topic are given; for example, topic-location-period versus location-topic-period.

CLA. Canadian Library Association.

Closed entry. Catalog record previously containing open dates, etc., for a publication in progress, that has been completed or "closed," presumably because the title is completed, for example, the fourth volume received that completes a four-volume set. *See also* Open entry.

Coding. The act or process of assigning MARC content designators to bibliographic data. Sometimes called *coding and tagging. See also* Tagging.

Collocate. To bring related items together, such as titles written by the same author, editions and versions of the same title, or materials on the same topic.

Colophon. A page at the end of a printed item on which bibliographic information is given.

Content designators. In the MARC formats, all of the characters or combinations of characters identifying specific parts of bibliographic, authority, community information, or holdings records, and the kinds of data held in them.

Continuation. A publication such as a serial, series, or frequently revised monographic title to which a library or information center subscribes on an ongoing basis.

Control field. A field in the MARC format identified by a tag beginning with the number zero. Control fields contain information such as call number, ISBN, LCCN, etc. *See also* Fixed field, Variable field.

Controlled vocabulary. A list of terms authorized for indexing, such as a subject heading list or thesaurus. *See also* Subject authority.

Conventional title. *See* Uniform title.

Copy cataloging/classification. A method of cataloging or classifying library materials in which a source record is copied or edited instead of creating a new record. Also called "derived cataloging/classification." *See also* Original cataloging/classification.

Core record. A catalog record standard containing less data than that required for full-level status by national bibliographic input standards, but more than that required for minimal-level status. Core records include, in addition to minimal-level data, selected descriptive fields and access points that conform fully to national authority control requirements. *See also* PCC.

Corporate body. A named group of people that acts as an entity.

Cross-reference. A message in the catalog that links two or more related access points, for example, a message at *Clemens, Samuel Langhorne* referring searchers to *Twain, Mark*.

CSB. *See Cataloging Service Bulletin.*

CSH. *See Canadian Subject Headings.*

Cutter letter(s). Alphabetic device similar to a cutter number in which one or more letters are used in place of combined letters and numbers to arrange items in alphabetical order. *See also* Cutter number, Shelf mark.

Cutter number. An alphanumeric code originated by Charles A. Cutter, designed to arrange items in alphabetical order. Sometimes called "book mark" or "book number." *See also* Shelf mark.

Cuttered, cuttering, cutters. Forms of the word "cutter" used as a verb, meaning the act of assigning cutter numbers.

DDC. Dewey decimal classification.

De facto. Literally meaning "in fact" or "in practice." A term applied to the Library of Congress functioning in the role of national library of the United States even though no legislation designates it as such.

Delimiter. In the MARC format, a symbol identifying the start of a subfield. Delimiters can print variously as double daggers, dollar signs, "at" symbols, vertical lines, or other characters. *See also* Subfield code.

Derived cataloging/classification. *See* Copy cataloging/classification. *See also* Original cataloging/classification.

Descriptor. A term consisting of one or more words indicating subject matter, often taken from a list of terms known as a thesaurus or subject heading list. *See also* Subject authority, Subject heading.

Dictionary catalog. A catalog in which all records are filed alphabetically. *See also* Divided catalog.

Direct entry. (1) An access point in which the desired name or word is the first part of the heading without naming a larger unit of which it is part. For example, KENTUCKY, not UNITED STATES—KENTUCKY. (2) A multiword heading given in the order in which it would be spoken (that is, the "natural order") without reversing the order of the words. For example, LIBRARY CATALOGS, not CATALOGS, LIBRARY. *See also* Indirect entry. (3) A corporate body name heading for a part of a larger body that is entered under its own name, not the name of the large body. For example, LIBRARY OF CONGRESS, not UNITED STATES LIBRARY OF CONGRESS.

Divided catalog. A catalog in which different types of records are gathered into separate files; for example, author headings in one file, title headings in a second file, and subject headings in a third file; or, author and title headings in one file, topical subject headings in a separate file. *See also* Dictionary catalog.

Downloading. The act of transmitting data electronically from a large computer database to a smaller local computer system. *See also* Uploading.

Emanate/emanation. To issue/the issuing of items by a corporate body.

Entry. Narrowly defined, an access point; broadly defined, a bibliographic record.

Extent. The total amount of an item's physical manifestation; for example, the pages of a book.

Field. In the MARC formats, one part of a record corresponding to one area of description, one subject heading, one call number, etc. *See also* Control field, Fixed field, Variable field.

Fixed field. (1) Any field containing data of fixed length and in fixed format. For example, the 043 field contains codes representing geographic data given in eye-readable form elsewhere in the record: "na us ca" in the 043 field stands for "North America-United States-California." (2) In OCLC records, this refers also to special formatting of the 008 field, in which specially designed prefixes identify subfields in place of the usual subfield codes. *See also* Control field, Variable field.

Form subdivision. In subject cataloging or indexing, a term used as a subdivision that describes the form or genre of an item, such as "—DICTIONARIES"; in classification, a number or span of numbers assigned to materials having specific forms or genres; for example, in DDC, standard subdivision "-05" means Serials.

Free-floating subdivision. In subject authorities, a term that can be added to authorized subject terms as a subdivision without a specific listing or instruction.

Full stop. British term for the mark of punctuation called a period by North Americans.

Heading. *See* Access point.

IFLA. International Federation of Library Associations and Institutions.

Imprint. Publishing data for a book, including the location and name of the publisher and the date of publication. In AACR2, these data were expanded and renamed "publication, distribution, etc.," information.

Indicators. In MARC format fields, special values that instruct the computer to manipulate data in a particular way. For example, in the 245 field, the first indicator value controls making an added entry for the title proper and the second indicator value controls indexing of the title proper.

Indirect entry. An access point, often a geographic or corporate body name, in which the desired name is not the first part of the heading; for example, the desired name is REFERENCE AND ADULT SERVICES DIVISION, but the heading is AMERICAN LIBRARY ASSOCIATION. REFERENCE AND ADULT SERVICES DIVISION. *See also* Direct entry.

Indirect subdivision. A subdivision of an access point in which the subdividing term is expressed indirectly; for example, the indirect subdivision of the subject heading for hotels in Edinburgh, Scotland, would be HOTELS—SCOTLAND—EDINBURGH, not HOTELS—EDINBURGH.

International Standard Bibliographic Description. *See* ISBD.

International Standard Book Number. *See* ISBN.

ISBD. International Standard Bibliographic Description. An international standard promulgated by IFLA for describing materials, which mandates sources for the descriptive data, the data elements, the order in which they are to appear, and punctuation to identify them.

ISBN. International Standard Book Number. An internationally used unique identifier for each title issued by publishers participating in the program.

ISSN. International Standard Serial Number. An internationally accepted number for the unique identification of serial publications.

Joint Steering Committee for Revision of AACR. An international body consisting of representatives of the library associations and national libraries of the United States (that is, the Library of Congress), Canada, the United Kingdom, and Australia, charged with determining the contents of the *Anglo-American Cataloguing Rules.* Also called "Joint Steering Committee" and abbreviated JSC. Superseded by the Joint Steering Committee for Development of RDA.

Joint Steering Committee for Development of RDA. An international body consisting of representatives of the library associations and national libraries of the United States (that is, the Library of Congress), Canada, the United Kingdom, and Australia, charged with developing the contents of the *Resource Description and Access.* Also called "Joint Steering Committee" and abbreviated JSC. Supersedes the Joint Steering Committee for Revision of AACR.

JSC. *See* Joint Steering Committee for Revision of AACR; Joint Steering Committee for Development of RDA.

LAC. Library and Archives of Canada. Formerly known as National Library of Canada.

LCC. Library of Congress Classification.

LCCN. Library of Congress Control Number. A unique number assigned by the Library of Congress to each catalog record it creates and by which its customers order cataloging on cards or in computer-readable format. Before the advent of computerized cataloging products, the acronym stood for Library of Congress Card Number.

LCSH. *Library of Congress Subject Headings.* A subject authority produced by the Library of Congress.

Leaves. Pages printed on one side only.

Local system. A computer system entirely within the control of a single library or library system. A local system can be shared by a small group of libraries.

Main class. In classification, the primary categories into which knowledge is divided.

Main entry. (1) The first and most important descriptive access point assigned to a catalog record by which the item can be retrieved. (2) In a single entry catalog, the access point for a record.

MARC. MAchine-Readable Cataloging. A group of identifying codes used to communicate bibliographic and other types of data using computers; originally devised by the Library of Congress.

MARC formats. The compilation(s) of codes used for identifying data for computer communication. Formats have been established for bibliographic data, authorities, holdings, classification, and community information. *See also* MARC.

MARC 21. A version of the MARC format that merges previously separate formats used by the Library of Congress (USMARC) and the National Library of Canada (CAN/MARC).

Metadata. Information used for identification and retrieval of electronic resources, similar to cataloging for books and other analog materials.

Minimal level cataloging. Catalog records containing less information than the minimum required by currently accepted standards.

Mixed notation. In classification, a system of symbols representing the subjects composed of more than one type of character; for example, numbers and letters of the alphabet as found in the Library of Congress classification. *See also* Pure notation.

Mixed responsibility. An item created by differing contributions of more than one responsible party, such as a book having an author, an editor, and an illustrator.

Monograph. An item published or produced in full within a finite time period.

Monographic series. *See* Series.

NAF. Name Authority File.

Name authority. An official record of the establishment of a name form for use as an access point in library catalogs, with its cross-references and data sources. *See also* Authority record.

NLC. *See* LAC.

OCLC. Online Computer Library Center. A bibliographic utility headquartered in Dublin, Ohio, and formerly known as the Ohio College Library Center.

Online Computer Library Center. *See* OCLC.

OPAC. Online Public Access Catalog. *See also* PAC.

Open entry. Catalog record for a publication-in-progress in which selected elements are left incomplete, such as dates and extent of the item; for example, a five-volume set of encyclopedias for which only a few of the volumes have been received. *See also* Closed entry.

Original cataloging/classification. The process of creating a new catalog record for an item without the use of a previously created record for the same or a related item. *See also* Copy cataloging/classification.

Other physical details. Data relating to the physical properties of an item being cataloged other than its extent, dimensions, and accompanying materials. For example, for a book, it includes illustrations; for an electronic resource, it includes the presence of sound, color, etc.

Other preliminaries. *See* Preliminaries.

Other title information. Title information other than the main title (the title proper), alternative title (a title following the title proper preceded by the word "or"), and parallel title (the title proper in another language or script).

Outsourcing. The practice of contracting with an organization outside the library or media center, often but not always a commercial organization, for operations or services typically performed within the library or media center, such as cataloging.

PAC. Public Access Catalog. *See also* OPAC.

Parallel title. The main title of an item in another language or script.

Parenthetic qualifier. *See* Qualifier.

Pattern heading. In *Library of Congress Subject Headings*, a set of subdivisions for a subject heading designated to be applied to all other subject headings of the same type without additional instruction. *See also* Key heading.

PCC. Program for Cooperative Cataloging; sponsor of the core record standard.

Preliminaries. Pages in a book beginning with the cover and concluding with the verso of the title page. Also called "other preliminaries" to exclude the title page recto from the definition.

Prescribed source(s). Location(s) authorized by AACR2-2005 for obtaining bibliographic data for a particular area of description. The locations vary by type of material. *See also* Chief source.

Primary entry. *See* Main entry.

Pure notation. In classification, a system of symbols representing subjects that use only one type of character; for example, only digits (as in DDC) or only letters of the Roman alphabet. *See also* Mixed notation.

Qualifier. A word or phrase that removes ambiguity from an access point, usually given in parentheses; for example, Cambridge (Mass.) and Cambridge (England), or Kiss (Performing group).

Recto. The right-hand page of a book, always bearing an odd number. *See also* Verso.

Retrieval point. *See* Access point.

RTSD. Resources and Technical Services Division of the American Library Association. Former name of the division known since 1990 as Association for Library Collections & Technical Services (ALCTS).

Rule of Three. A library rule-of-thumb using three as the cutoff point for differing treatments: (1) in AACR-2005, if one, two, or three authors are equally responsible for an item, choose the first named as the main entry, but if there are more than three, choose the title as the main entry; (2) in *Sears List of Subject Headings*, suggestion that not more than three subject headings should be applied to one item.

SAC. Subject Analysis Committee of the Cataloging and Classification Section of the Association for Library Collections & Technical Services. This committee is responsible for monitoring issues and standards used in subject cataloging and classification.

Secondary entry. *See* Added entry.

Separate bibliographic identity. *See* Bibliographic identity.

Serial. An item published or produced in parts intended to go on without end. Should not be confused with *series.*

Series. A group of discrete items having, in addition to their own titles, a common title identifying them as part of the group. Also called *monographic series.* Should not be confused with *serial.*

Set. A group of related materials that can be cataloged as a group.

Shared responsibility. Applies when an item is created by more than one responsible party sharing the same type of contribution; for example, a book with multiple authors.

Shelf mark. Any code or system of marks designed to arrange items on shelves, excluding the classification numbers; also called book mark or call letter. *See also* Cutter letter, Cutter number.

Shelf list. A catalog of items owned by a library arranged by call number.

Specificity. The degree of broadness or narrowness of a term used for indexing materials; or, the degree of broadness or narrowness of a subject catalog.

Standard number. *See* ISBN.

Standard subdivision. In the Dewey decimal classification, a number from auxiliary Table 1 that can be added to a number from the schedules without a specific instruction to do so.

Statement of responsibility. Part of the first area of description naming those with overall responsibility for the creation of the item.

Subfield. Part of a field in the MARC format.

Subfield code. A character identifying the subfield and the data it contains. *See also* Delimiter.

Subject authority. A record documenting the establishment of an acceptable subject term containing the term, the cross-references established with it, and the sources of the information. *See also* Controlled vocabulary.

Subject cataloging. The act of assigning subject headings to an item being cataloged.

Subject heading. (1) A word or phrase identifying the intellectual content of an item being cataloged and used as an access point. (2) A term from an authorized list of terms to be used as access points. *See also* Descriptor.

Subject heading list. A list of terms, usually including cross-references, for indexing items being cataloged. Subject heading lists usually cover all branches of knowledge unless they explicitly state otherwise. *See also* Thesaurus.

Subordinate entry. The listing of a part of a corporate body under the name of the parent body.

Tag. The three-digit code identifying a field in the MARC format.

Tagging. The act of assigning codes to bibliographic data in the MARC format. Also known as *tagging and coding. See also* Coding.

Thesaurus. A list of terms with cross-references that clarify the relationships among terms used for indexing. Thesauri often are limited to a single discipline or group of disciplines. *See also* Subject heading list.

Title proper. The main title of an item.

Uniform title. A title created and assigned by catalogers to collocate editions and versions of a work that appear under different titles proper. The uniform title assigned to an item may be the title by which it is commonly known, the original title of a work published in translation, or a title constructed by the cataloger.

Uploading. The act of transmitting data electronically from a small local computer system to a larger computer database. *See also* Downloading.

Utility. *See* Bibliographic utility.

Variable field. A field in the MARC format containing data that varies in length and format. *See also* Control field, Fixed field.

Verso. (1) Left-hand page of a book, always bearing an even number. (2) Back of the title page.

Indexes

The two indexes that follow provide a detailed guide to the contents of the book. The first index is a topical guide to the text. The second index accommodates those who wish to study the figures and examples more systematically, and is divided into four subsections: Type of Media, Access Points, Description, and Classification/Call Numbers. Problems encountered in normal cataloging can be checked across figures and examples using these indexes. This should provide valuable additional practice in learning the rules.

TOPICAL INDEX TO THE TEXT

INDEX TO FIGURES AND EXAMPLES

TYPE OF MEDIA

ACCESS POINTS

DESCRIPTION

CLASSIFICATION/CALL NUMBERS

About the Authors

In her long career, JEAN WEIHS has worked in university, public, school, and special libraries as a reference librarian, a bibliographer, and a school librarian. Most of her career, however, she has been involved in cataloging, as both a practitioner and a teacher of librarians, library technicians, and school librarians in Canada, where she served as Director of the Library Techniques Program at Seneca College of Applied Arts and Technology until her retirement in 1986. Subsequent to this, she taught as a visiting professor at UCLA and Simmons College and acted as a consultant. She represented the Canadian Committee on Cataloguing for nine years on the Joint Steering Committee for Revision of AACR, five of these as JSC Chair. She has held forty-five positions on national and international committees. Among the many publications for which she is a principal author or editor are four editions of *Nonbook Materials: The Organization of Integrated Collections* (one of the books that was used as the basis for formulating rules in AACR2 for these materials; published 1970, 1973, 1979, and 1989); *Accessible Storage of Nonbook Materials* (1984) and its second edition, *The Integrated Library* (1991); *The Principles and Future of AACR: Proceedings of the International Conference on the Principles and Future Development of AACR* (1998); and three editions of *Standard Cataloging for School and Public Libraries*. She is the recipient of many honors, including the prestigious Margaret Mann Citation Award sponsored by the Cataloging and Classification Section of the Association for Library Collections & Technical Services, University of Toronto Faculty of Library and Information Science 60th Anniversary Award for outstanding contributions to the field of library and information science, the Queen's Jubilee Medal (given by the Governor General of Canada, nominated by the Canadian Library Association), the Online Audiovisual Catalogers' Nancy B. Olson Award for lifetime achievement in the development of access to media collections, and the Canadian Association of College and University Libraries' Blackwell's Award for Distinguished Academic Librarian.

SHEILA S. INTNER is Professor Emerita in the Simmons College Graduate School of Library and Information Science. She was the founding director of Simmons' MLIS program at Mount Holyoke College, established in 2001, and is currently adjunct professor at the College of Library and Information Science at the University of Maryland. She has been teaching library organization and collections management since 1980 and has been involved in the development of organizational standards since 1989, when she was simultaneously

183

elected an American Library Association Councilor-at-large and president of the Association for Library Collections & Technical Services, the association most closely associated with metadata and cataloging standards. She has received numerous awards, including the prestigious Margaret Mann Citation Award for outstanding contributions to education for cataloging and classification, and the Online Audiovisual Catalogers' Annual Award for excellence in promoting standards in online cataloging. She is the author or principal editor of twenty-two books, including *Electronic Cataloging* (2003), *Cataloging Correctly for Kids* (American Library Association, 2006), *Metadata and Its Impact on Libraries* (Libraries Unlimited, 2006), and the first three editions of *Standard Cataloging for School and Public Libraries* (Libraries Unlimited, 1994, 1998, and 2001).